# Ambedkar's India

## A Collection of 3 Works

Bhimrao Ambedkar

# Ambedkar's India

A Collection of 3 Works

Bhimrao Ambedkar

Political Science

**Edited,** Printed & Published by:
Jagath Jayaprakash

First Published:
March 2023

Copyright © 2023 Jagath Jayaprakash

All rights reserved. No part of this publication may be reproduced, stored or transmitted in any form or by any means, electronic, mechanical, photocopying, recording, scanning, or otherwise, without written permission from the publisher. It is illegal to copy this book, post it to a website, or distribute it by any other means without permission.

**Honest Books**
Geethalayam
Pattamthuruthu,
Kollam-691601
Kerala, India
Phone: +91 8075374584

Email id: jagathjp86@gmail.com

# Contents

| | |
|---|---|
| EDITORS NOTE | iii |
| THE GRAMMAR OF ANARCHY | 1 |
| CASTES IN INDIA: THEIR MECHANISM, GENESIS, AND DEVELOPMENT | 15 |
| ANNIHILATION OF CASTE | 33 |
| ABOUT THE AUTHOR | 107 |

# Editor's Note

Ambedkar's India is a compilation of three of B.R. Ambedkar's most renowned addresses on caste and the Indian Constitution.

"The Grammar of Anarchy" is a speech he made while presenting the draft Constitution before the Constituent Assembly on November 4, 1948. It demonstrates how he believed we should pave the path for India's independence, discusses the work of the Constituent Assembly, and outlines the Constitution's social, political and economic philosophy. Furthermore, it demonstrates his affection for India and its people and his aspirations for their future.

The article "Castes in India: Their Mechanism, Genesis, and Development" was a presentation by B. R. Ambedkar on May 9, 1916, at Alexander Goldenweiser's anthropological seminar in New York. It was subsequently published in May 1917 in the issue XLI of Indian Antiquary. It describes in depth how classes in India's social order evolved into castes and sub-castes.

"Annihilation of Caste" is an undelivered speech prepared in 1936 for a convention of liberal Hindu caste reformers in Lahore. It is one of Ambedkar's finest works since it demonstrates how the caste system has eroded the foundations of a multicultural nation like India.


Jagath Jayaprakash

20/03/2023

# THE GRAMMAR OF ANARCHY

A speech delivered by B R Ambedkar while presenting the draft Constitution before the assembly on November 4, 1948

# THE GRAMMAR OF ANARCHY

**The Honourable Dr. B. R. Ambedkar*** : Sir, looking back on the work of the Constituent Assembly it will now be two years, eleven months and seventeen days since it first met on the 9th of December 1946. During this period the Constituent Assembly has altogether held eleven sessions. Out of these eleven sessions the first six were spent in passing the Objectives Resolution and the consideration of the Reports of Committees on Fundamental Rights, on Union Constitution, on Union Powers, on Provincial Constitution, on Minorities and on the Scheduled Areas and Scheduled Tribes. The seventh, eighth, ninth, tenth and the eleventh sessions were devoted to the consideration of the Draft Constitution. These eleven sessions of the Constitutent Assembly have consumed 165 days. Out of these, the Assembly spent 114 days for the consideration of the Draft Constitution.

Coming to the Drafting Committee, it was elected by the Constituent Assembly on 29th August 1947. It held its first meeting on 30th August. Since August 30th it sat for 141 days during which it was engaged in the preparation of the Draft Constitution. The Draft Constitution, as prepared by the Constitutional Adviser as a text for the Drafting Committee to work upon, consisted of 243 articles and 13 Schedules. The first Draft Constitution as presented by the Drafting Committee to the Constituent Assembly contained 315 articles and 8 Schedules. At the end of the consideration stage, the number of articles in the Draft Constitution increased to 386. In its final form, the Draft Constitution contains 395 articles and 8 Schedules. The total number of amendments to the Draft Constitution tabled was approximately 7,635. Of them, the total number of amendments actually moved in the house were 2,473.

I mention these facts because at one stage it was being said that the Assembly had taken too long a time to finish its work, that it was going on leisurely and wasting public money. It was said to be a case of Nero fiddling while Rome was burning. Is there any justification for this complaint ? Let us note the time consumed by Constituent Assemblies in other countries appointed for framing their Constitutions. To take a few illustrations, the American Convention met on May 25th, 1787 and completed its work on September 17, 1787 *i.e.,* within four months. The

---
*CAD, Official Report, Vol. X, 25th November 1949, pp. 972-981.

Constitutional Convention of Canada met on the 10th October 1864 and the Constitution was passed into law in March 1867 involving a period of two years and five months. The Australian Constitutional Convention assembled in March 1891 and the Constitution became law on the 9th July 1900, consuming a period of nine years. The South African Convention met in October 1908 and the Constitution became law on the 20th September 1909 involving one year's labour. It is true that we have taken more time than what the American or South African Conventions did. But we have not taken more time than the Canadian Convention and much less than the Australian Convention. In making comparisons on the basis of time consumed, two things must be remembered. One is that the Constitutions of America, Canada, South Africa and Australia are much smaller than ours. Our Constitution, as I said, contains 395 articles while the American has just seven articles, the first four of which are divided into sections which total up to 21, the Canadian has 147, Australian 128 and South African 153 sections. The second thing to be remembered is that the makers of the Constitutions of America, Canada, Australia and South Africa did not have to face the problem of amendments. They were passed as moved. On the other hand, this Constituent Assembly had to deal with as many as 2,473 amendments. Having regard to these facts the charge of dilatoriness seems to me quite unfounded and this Assembly may well congratualate itself for having accomplished so formidable a task in so short a time.

Turning to the quality of the work done by the Drafting Committee, Mr. Naziruddin Ahmed felt it his duty to condemn it outright. In his opinion, the work done by the Drafting Committee is not only not worthy of commendation, but is positively below par. Everybody has a right to have his opinion about the work done by the Drafting Committee and Mr. Naziruddin is welcome to have his own. Mr. Naziruddin Ahmed thinks he is a man of greater talents than any member of the Drafting Committee. The Drafting Committee does not wish to challenge his claim. On the other hand, the Drafting Committee would have welcomed him in their midst if the Assembly had thought him worthy of being appointed to it. If he had no place in the making of the Constitution it is certainly not the fault of the Drafting Committee.

Mr. Naziruddin Ahmad has coined a new name for the Drafting Committee evidently to show his contempt for it. He calls it a Drifting Committee. Mr. Naziruddin must no doubt be pleased with his hit. But he evidently does not know that there is a difference between drift without mastery and drift with mastery. If the Drafting Committee was drifting, it was never without mastery over the situation. It was not merely angling with the off chance of catching a fish. It was searching in known waters to find the fish it was after. To be in search of something better is not the same as drifting. Although Mr. Naziruddin Ahmad did not mean it as a compliment to the Drafting Committee, I take it as a compliment to the Drafting Committee. The Drafting Committee would have been guilty of gross dereliction of duty and of a false sense of dignity if it had not shown the honesty and the courage to withdraw the amendments which it thought faulty and substitute what it thought was better. If it is a mistake, I am glad the Drafting Committee did not fight shy of admitting such mistakes and coming forward to correct them.

I am glad to find that with the exception of a solitary member, there is a general consensus of appreciation from the members of the Constituted Assembly of the work done by the Drafting Committee. I am sure the Drafting Committee feels happy to find this spontaneous recognition of its labours expressed in such generous terms. As to the compliments that have been showered upon me both by the members of the Assembly as well as by my colleagues of the Drafting Committee I feel so overwhelmed that I cannot find adequate words to express fully my gratitude to them. I came into the Constituent Assembly with no greater aspiration than to safeguard the interests of the Scheduled Castes. I had not the remotest idea that I would be called upon to undertake more responsible functions. I was therefore greatly surprised when the Assembly elected me to the Drafting Committee. I was more than surprised when the Drafting Committee elected me to be its Chairman. There were in the Drafting Committee men bigger, better and more competent than myself such as my friend Sir Alladi Krishnaswami Ayyar. I am grateful to the Constituent Assembly and the Drafting Committee for reposing in me so much trust and confidence and to have chosen me as their instrument and given me this opportunity of serving the country. *(Cheers.)*

The credit that is given to me does not really belong to me. It belongs partly to Sir B. N. Rau, the Constitutional Adviser to the Constituent Assembly who prepared a rough draft of the Constitution for the consideration of the Drafting Committee. A part of the credit must go to the members of the Drafting Committee who, as I have said, have sat for 141 days and without whose ingenuity to devise new formulae and capacity to tolerate and to accommodate different points of view, the task of framing the Constitution could not have come to so successful a conclusion. Much greater share of the credit must go to Mr. S. N. Mukherjee, the Chief Draftsman of the Constitution. His ability to put the most intricate proposals in the simplest and clearest legal form can rarely be equalled, nor his capacity for hard work. He has been an acquisition to the Assembly. Without his help, this Assembly would have taken many more years to finalise the Constitution. I must not omit to mention the members of the staff working under Mr. Mukherjee, for, I know how hard they have worked and how long they have toiled, sometimes even beyond midnight. I want to thank them all for their effort and their co-operation. *(cheers.)*

The task of the Drafting Committee would have been a very difficult one if this Constituent Assembly has been merely a motely crowd, a tasseleted pavement without cement, a black stone here and a white stone there in which each member or each group was a law unto itself. There would have been nothing but chaos. This possibility of chaos was reduced to nil by the existence of the Congress Party inside the Assembly which brought into its proceedings a sense of order and discipline. It is because of the discipline of the Congress Party that the Drafting Committee was able to pilot the Constitution in the Assembly with the sure knowledge as to the fate of each article and each amendment. The Congress Party is, therefore, entitled to all the credit for the smooth sailing of the Draft Constitution in the Assembly.

The proceedings of this Constituent Assembly would have been very dull if all members had yielded to the rule of party discipline. Party discipline, in all its rigidity, would have converted this Assembly into a gathering of 'yes' men. Fortunately, there were rebels. They were Mr. Kamath, Dr. P. S. Deshmukh, Mr. Sidhva, Prof. Sexena and Pandit Thakur Das Bhargava. Along with them I must mention Prof. K. T. Shah and Pandit Hirday Nath Kunzru. The points they raised were mostly ideological. That I was not prepared to accept their suggestions, does not diminish the value of their suggestions nor lessen the service they have rendered to the Assembly in enlivening its proceedings. I am grateful to them. But for them, I would not have had the opportunity which I got for expounding the principles underlying the Constitution which was more important than the mere mechanical work of passing the Constitution.

Finally, I must thank you Mr. President for the way in which you have conducted the proceedings of this Assembly. The courtesy and the consideration which you have shown to the Members of the Assembly can never be forgotten by those who have taken part in the proceedings of this Assembly. There were occasions when the amendments of the Drafting Committee were sought to be barred on grounds purely technical in their nature. Those were very anxious moments for me. I am, therefore, specially grateful to you for not permitting legalism to defeat the work of Constitution-making.

As much defence as could be offered to the Constitution has been offered by my friends Sir Alladi Krishnaswami Ayyar and Mr. T. T. Krishnamachari. I shall not therefore enter into the merits of the Constitution. Because I feel, however good a Constitution may be, it is sure to turn out bad because those who are called to work it, happen to be a bad lot. However bad a Constitution may be, it may turn out to be good if those who are called to work it, happen to be a good lot. The working of a Constitution does not depend wholly upon the nature of the Constitution. The Constitution can provide only the organs of State such as the Legislature, the Executive and the Judiciary. The factors on which the working of those organs of the State depend are the people and the political parties they will set up as their instruments to carry out their wishes and their politics. Who can say how the people of India and their parties will behave? Will they uphold constitutional methods of achieving their purposes or will they prefer revolutionary methods of achieving them? If they adopt the revolutionary methods, however good the Constitution may be, it requires no prophet to say that it will fail. It is, therefore, futile to pass any judgment upon the Constitution without reference to the part which the people and their parties are likely to play.

The condemnation of the Constitution largely comes from two quarters, the Communist Party and the Socialist Party. Why do they condemn the Constitution? Is it because it is really a bad Constitution? I venture to say 'no.' The Communist Party wants a Constitution based upon the principle of the Dictatorship of the Proletariat. They condemn the Constitution because it is based upon parliamentary democracy. The Socialists want two things. The first thing they want is that if they come in power, the Constitution must give them the freedom to nationalize or socialize all private property without payment of compensation. The second thing that the Socialists want is that the Fundamental Rights mentioned in the Constitution must be absolute and without any limitations so that if their Party fails to come into power, they would have the unfettered freedom not merely to criticize, but also to overthrow the State.

These are the main grounds on which the Constitution is being condemned. I do not say that the principle of parliamentary democracy is the only ideal form of political democracy. I do not say that the principle of no acquisition of private property without compensation is so sacrosanct that there can be no departure from it. I do not say that Fundamental Rights can never be absolute and the limitations set upon them can never be lifted. What I do say is that the principles embodied in the Constitution are the views of the present generation or if you think this to be an overstatement, I say they are the views of the members of the Constituent Assembly. Why blame the Drafting Committee for embodying them in the Constitution? I say why blame even the Members of the Constituent Assembly? Jefferson, the great American statesman who played so great a part in the making of the American Constitution, has expressed some very weighty views which makers of Constitution, can never afford to ignore. In one place, he has said :—

> "We may consider each generation as a distinct nation, with a right, by the will of the majority, to bind themselves, but none to bind the succeeding generation, more than the inhabitants of another country."

In another place, he has said :

> "The idea that institutions established for the use of the nation cannot be touched or modified, even to make them answer their end, because of rights gratuitously supposed in those employed to manage them in the trust for the public, may perhaps be a salutary provision against the abuses of a monarch, but is most absurd against the nation itself, Yet our lawyers and priests generally inculcate this doctrine, and suppose that preceding generations held the earth more freely than we do; had a right to impose laws on us, unalterable by ourselves, and that we, in the like manner, can make laws and impose burdens on future generations, which they will have no right to alter; in fine, that the earth belongs to the dead and not the living;"

I admit that what Jefferson has said is not merely true, but is absolutely true. There can be no question about it. Had the Constitutent Assembly departed from this principle laid down by Jefferson it would certainly be liable to blame, even to condemnation. But I ask, has it? Quite the contrary. One has only to examine the provision relating to the amendment of the Constitution. The Assembly has not only refrained from putting a seal of finality and infallibility upon this Constitution by denying to the people the right to amend the Constitution as in Canada or by making the amendment of the Constitution subject to the fulfilment of extraordinary terms and conditions as in America or Australia, but has provided a most facile procedure for amending the Constitution. I challenge any of the critics of the Constitution to prove that any Constituent

Assembly anywhere in the world has, in the circumstances in which this country finds itself, provided such a facile procedure for the amendment of the Constitution. If those who are dissatisfied with the Constitution have only to obtain a 2/3 majority and if they cannot obtain even a two-third majority in the parliament elected on adult franchise in their favour, their dissatisfaction with the Constitution cannot be deemed to be shared by the general public.

There is only one point of constitutional import to which I propose to make a reference. A serious complaint is made on the ground that there is too much of centralization and that the States have been reduced to Municipalities. It is clear that this view is not only an exaggeration, but is also founded on a misunderstanding of what exactly the Constitution contrives to do. As to the relation between the Centre and the States, it is necessary to bear in mind the fundamental principle on which it rests. The basic principle of Federalism is that the Legislative and Executive authority is partitioned between the Centre and the States not by any law to be made by the Centre but by the Constitution itself. This is what Constitution does. The States under our Constitution are in no way dependent upon the Centre for their legislative or executive authority. The Centre and the States are co-equal in this matter. It is difficult to see how such a Constitution can be called centralism. It may be that the Constitution assigns to the Centre too large a field for the operation of its legislative and executive authority than is to be found in any other federal Constitution. It may be that the residuary powers are given to the Centre and not to the States. But these features do not form the essence of federalism. The chief mark of federalism as I said lies in the partition of the legislative and executive authority between the Centre and the Units by the Constitution. This is the principle embodied in our Constitution. There can be no mistake about it. It is, therefore, wrong to say that the States have been placed under the Centre. Centre cannot by its own will alter the boundary of that partition. Nor can the Judiciary. For as has been well said :

> "Courts may modify, they cannot replace. They can revise earlier interpretations as new arguments, new points of view are presented, they can shift the dividing line in marginal cases, but there are barriers they cannot pass, definite assignments of power they cannot reallocate. They can give a broadening construction of existing powers, but they cannot assign to one authrority powers explicitly granted to another."

The first charge of centralisation defeating federalism must therefore fall.

The second charge is that the Centre has been given the power to override the States. This charge must be admitted. But before condemning the Constitution for containing such overriding powers, certain considerations must be borne in mind. The first is that these overriding powers do not form the normal feature of the Constitution. Their use and operation are expressly confined to emergencies only. The second consideration is: Could we avoid giving overriding powers to the Centre when an emergency has arisen? Those who do not admit the justification for such overriding powers to the Centre even in an emergency, do not seem to have a clear idea of the problem which lies at the root of the matter. The problem is so clearly set out by a writer in that wellknown magazine "The Round Table" in its issue of December 1935 that I offer no apology for quoting the following extract from it. Says the writer:

> "Political systems are a complex of rights and duties resting ultimately on the question, to whom, or to what authority, does the citizen owe allegiance. In normal affairs the question is not present, for the law works smoothly, and a man goes about his business obeying one authority in this set of matters and another authority in that. But in a moment of crisis, a conflict of claims may arise, and it is then apparent that ultimate allegiance cannot be divided. The issue of allegiance cannot be determined in the last resort by a juristic interpretation of statutes. The law must conform to the facts or so much the worse for the law. When all formalism is stripped away, the bare question is, what authority commands the residual loyalty of the citizen, Is it the Centre or the Constituent State?"

The solution of this problem depends upon one's answer to this question which is the crux of the problem. There can be no doubt that in the opinion of the vast majority of the people, the residual loyalty of the citizen in an emergency must be to the Centre and not to the Constituent States. For it is only the Centre which can work for a common end and for the general interests of the country as a whole. Herein lies the justification for giving to the Centre certain overriding powers to be used in an emergency. And after all what is the obligation imposed upon the constituent States by these emergency powers? No more than this—that in an emergency, they should take into consideration alongside their own local interests, the opinions and interests of the nation as a whole. Only those who have not understood the problem, can complain against it.

Here I could have ended. But my mind is so full of the future of our country that I feel I ought to take this occasion to give expression to some of my reflections thereon. On 26th January 1950, India will be an independent country *(Cheers)*. What would happen to her independence? Will she maintain her independence or will she lose it again? This is the first thought that comes to my mind. It is not that India was never an independent country. The point is that she once lost the independence she had. Will she lose it a second time? It is this thought which makes me most anxious for the future. What perturbs me greatly is the fact that not only India has once before lost her independence, but she lost it by the infidelity and treachery of some of her own people. In the invasion of Sind by Mahommed-Bin-Kasim, the military commanders of King Dahar accepted bribes from the agents of Mahommed-Bin-Kasim and refused to fight on the side of their King. It was Jaichand who invited Mahommed Ghori to invade India and fight against Prithvi Raj and promised him the help of himself and the Solanki kings. When Shivaji was fighting for the liberation of Hindus, the other Maratha noblemen and the Rajput Kings were fighting the battle on the side of Moghul Emperors. When the British were trying to destroy the Sikh Rulers, Gulab Singh, their principal commander sat silent and did not help to save the Sikh kingdom. In 1857, when a large part of India had declared a war of independence against the British, the Sikhs stood and watched the event as silent spectators.

Will history repeat itself? It is this thought which fills me with anxiety. This anxiety is deepened by the realization of the fact that in addition to our old enemies in the form of castes and creeds we are going to have many political parties with diverse and opposing political creeds. Will Indians place the country above their creed or will they place creed above country? I do not know. But this much is certain that if the parties place creed above country, our independence will be put in jeopardy a second time and probably be lost for ever. This eventuality we must all resolutely guard against. We must be determined to defend our independence with the last drop of our blood. *(Cheers.)*

On the 26th of January 1950, India would be a democratic country in the sense that India from that day would have a government of the people, by the people and for the people. The same thought comes to my mind. What would happen to her democratic Constitution? Will she be able to maintain it or will she lose it again. This is the second thought that comes to my mind and makes me as anxious as the first.

It is not that India did not know what is Democracy. There was a time when India was studded with republics, and even where there were monarchies, they were either elected or limited. They were never absolute. It is not that India did not know Parliaments or Parliamentary Procedure. A study of the Buddhist Bhikshu Sanghas discloses that not only there were Parliaments—for the Sanghas were nothing but Parliaments—but the Sanghas knew and observed all the rules of Parliamentary Procedure known to modern times. They had rules regarding seating arrangements, rules regarding Motions, Resolutions, Quorum, Whip, Counting of Votes, Voting by Ballot, Censure Motion, Regularization, *Res Judicata,* etc. Although these rules of Parliamentary Procedure were applied by the Buddha to the meetings of the Sanghas, he must have borrowed them from the rules of the Political Assemblies functioning in the country in his time.

This democratic system India lost. Will she lose it a second time ? I do not know, but it is quite possible in a country like India—where democracy from its long disuse must be regarded as something quite new—there is danger of democracy giving place to dictatorship. It is quite possible for this new born democracy to retain its form but give place to dictatorship in fact. If there is a landslide, the danger of the second possibility becoming actuality is much greater.

If we wish to maintain democracy not merely in form, but also in fact, what must we do ? The first thing in my judgment we must do is to hold fast to constitutional methods of achieving our social and economic objectives. It means we must abandon the bloody methods of revolution. It means that we must abandon the method of civil disobedience, non-cooperation and satyagraha. When there was no way left for constitutional methods for achieving economic and social objectives, there was a great deal of justification for unconstitutional methods. But where constitutional methods are open, there can be no justification for these unconstitutional methods. These methods are nothing but the Grammar of Anarchy and the sooner they are abandoned, the better for us.

The second thing we must do is to observe the caution which John Stuart Mill has given to all who are interested in the maintenance of democracy, namely, not "to lay their liberties at the feet of even a great man, or to trust him with powers which enable him to subvert their institutions." There is nothing wrong in being grateful to great men who have rendered life-long services to the country. But there are limits to gratefulness. As has been well said by the Irish Patriot Daniel O'Connel, 'no man can be grateful at the cost of his honour, no woman can be grateful at the cost of her chastity and no nation can be grateful at the cost of its liberty.' This caution is far more necessary in the case of India than in the case of any other country, for in India, Bhakti or what may be called the path of devotion or hero-worship, plays a part in its politics unequalled in magnitude by the part it plays in the politics of any other country in the world. Bhakti in religion may be a road to the salvation of the soul. But in politics, Bhakti or hero-worship is a sure road to degradation and to eventual dictatorship.

The third thing we must do is not to be content with mere political democracy. We must make our political democracy a social democracy as well. Political democracy cannot last unless there lies at the base of it social democracy. What does social democracy mean ? It means a way of life which recognizes liberty, equality and fraternity as the principles of life. These principles of liberty, equality and fraternity are not to be treated as separate items in a trinity. They form a union of trinity in the sense that to divorce one from the other is to defeat the very purpose of democracy. Liberty cannot be divorced from equality, equality cannot be divorced from liberty. Nor can liberty and equality be divorced from fraternity. Without equality, liberty would produce the supremacy of the few over the many. Equality without liberty would kill individual initiative. Without fraternity, liberty and equality could not become a natural course of things. It would require a constable to enforce them. We must begin by acknowledging the fact that there is complete absence of two things in Indian Society. One of these is equality. On the social plane, we have in India a society based on the principle of graded inequality which means elevation for some and degradation for others. On the economic plane, we have a society in which there are some who have immense wealth as against many who live in abject poverty. On the 26th of January 1950, we are going to enter into a life of contradictions. In politics we will have equality and in social and economic life we will have inequality. In Politics we will be recognizing the principle of one man one vote and one vote one value. In our social and economic life, we shall, by reason of our social and economic structure, continue to deny the principle of one man one value. How long shall we continue to live this life of contradictions ? How long shall we continue to deny equality in our social and economic life ? If we continue to deny it for long, we will do so only by putting our political democracy in peril. We must remove this contradiction at the earliest possible moment or else those who suffer from inequality will blow up the structure of political democracy which this Assembly has so laboriously built up.

The second thing we are wanting in is recognition of the principle of fraternity. What does fraternity mean ? Fraternity means a sense of common brotherhood of all Indians—if Indians being one people. It is the principle which gives unity and solidarity to social life. It is a difficult thing to achieve. How difficult it is, can be realized from the story related by James Bryce in his volume on American Commnowealth about the United States of America.

The story is—I propose to recount it in the words of Bryce himself—that—

> "Some years ago the American Protestant Episcopal Church was occupied at its triennial convention in revising its liturgy. It was thought desirable to introduce among the short sentence prayers a prayer for the whole people, and an eminent New England divine proposed the words 'O Lord, bless our nation'. Accepted one afternoon on the spur of the moment, the sentence was brought up next day for reconsideration, when so many objections were raised by the laity to the word 'nation' as importing too definite a recognition of national unity, that it was dropped, and instead there were adopted the words 'O Lord, bless these United States'."

There was so little solidarity in the U.S.A. at the time when this incident occurred that the people of America did not think that they were a nation. If the people of the United States could not feel that they were a nation, how difficult it is for Indians to think that they are a nation. I remember the days when politically-minded Indians resented the expression "the people of India". They preferred the expression "the Indian nation." I am of opinion that in believing that we are a nation, we are cherishing a great delusion. How can people divided into several thousands of castes be a nation? The sooner we realize that we are not as yet a nation in the social and psychological sense of the word, the better for us. For then only we shall realize the necessity of becoming a nation and seriously think of ways and means of realizing the goal. The realization of this goal is going to be very difficult—far more difficult than it has been in the United States. The United States has no caste problem. In India there are castes. The castes are anti-national. In the first place because they bring about separation in social life. They are anti-national also because they generate jealousy and antipathy between caste and caste. But we must overcome all these difficulties if we wish to become a nation in reality. For fraternity can be a fact only when there is a nation. Without fraternity, equality and liberty will be no deeper than coats of paint.

These are my reflections about me tasks that lie ahead of us. They may not be very pleasant to some. But there can be no gainsaying that political power in this country has too long been the monopoly of a few and the many are not only beasts of burden, but also beasts of prey. This monopoly has not merely deprived them of their chance of betterment, it has sapped them of what may be called the significance of life. These down-trodden classes are tired of being governed, they are impatient to govern themselves. This urge for self-realization in the downtrodden classes must not be allowed to develop into a class struggle or class war. It would lead to a division of the House. That would indeed be a day of disaster. For, as has been well said by Abraham Lincoln, a house divided against itself cannot stand very long. Therefore the sooner room is made for the realization of their aspiration, the better for the few, the better for the country, the better for the maintenance for its independence and the better for the continuance of its democratic structure. This can only be done by the establishment of equality and fraternity in all spheres of life. That is why I have laid so much stress on them.

I do not wish to weary the House any further. Independence is no doubt a matter of joy. But let us not forget that this independence has thrown on us great responsibilities. By independence, we have lost the excuse of blaming the British for anything going wrong. If hereafter things go wrong, we will have nobody to blame except ourselves. There is great danger of things going wrong. Times are fast changing. People including our own are being moved by new ideologies. They are getting tired of government by the people. They are prepared to have Government for the people and are indifferent whether it is Government of the people and by the people. If we wish to preserve the Constitution in which we have sought to enshrine the principle of Government of the people, for the people and by the people, let us resolve not to be tardy in the recognition of the evils that lie across our path and which induce people to prefer Government for the people to Government by the people, nor to be weak in our initiative to remove them. That is the only way to serve the country. I know of no better.

**Mr. President :** The House will adjourn till Ten of the clock tomorrow morning when we shall take up the voting on the motion which was moved by Dr. Ambedkar.

The Assembly then adjourned till ten of the Clock on Saturday, the 26th November, 1949.

\*     \*     \*     \*     \*

# CASTES IN INDIA
# THEIR MECHANISM, GENESIS, AND DEVELOPMENT

# CASTES IN INDIA

Many of us, I dare say, have witnessed local, national or international expositions of material objects that make up the sum total of human civilization. But few can entertain the idea of there being such a thing as an exposition of human institutions. Exhibition of human institutions is a strange idea; some might call it the wildest of ideas. But as students of Ethnology I hope you will not be hard on this innovation, for it is not so, and to you at least it should not be strange.

You all have visited, I believe, some historic place like the ruins of Pompeii, and listened with curiosity to the history of the remains as it flowed from the glib tongue of the guide. In my opinion a student of Ethnology, in one sense at least, is much like the guide. Like his prototype, he holds up (perhaps with more seriousness and desire of self-instruction) the social institutions to view, with all the objectiveness humanly possible, and inquires into their origin and function.

Most of our fellow students in this Seminar, which concerns itself with primitive *versus* modern society, have ably acquitted themselves along these lines by giving lucid expositions of the various institutions, modern or primitive, in which they are interested. It is my turn now, this evening, to entertain you, as best I can, with a paper on "*Castes in India* : Their mechanism, genesis and development"

I need hardly remind you of the complexity of the subject I intend to handle. Subtler minds and abler pens than mine have been brought to the task of unravelling the mysteries of Caste; but unfortunately it still remains in the domain of the "unexplained", not to say of the "un-understood" I am quite alive to the complex intricacies of a hoary institution like Caste, but I am not so pessimistic as to relegate it to the region of the unknowable, for I believe it can be known. The caste problem is a vast one, both theoretically and practically. Practically, it is an institution that portends tremendous consequences. It is a local problem, but one capable of much wider mischief, for "as long as caste in India does exist, Hindus will hardly intermarry or have any social intercourse with outsiders ; and if Hindus migrate to other regions on earth, Indian caste would become a world problem."[1] Theoretically, it has defied a great many scholars who have taken upon themselves, as a labour of love, to dig into its origin. Such being the case, I cannot treat the problem in its entirety. Time, space and acumen, I am afraid, would all fail me, if I attempted to do otherwise than limit myself to a phase of it, namely, the genesis, mechanism and spread of the caste system. I will strictly observe this rule, and will dwell on extraneous matters only when it is necessary to clarify or support a point in my thesis.

To proceed with the subject. According to well-known ethnologists, the population of India is a mixture of Aryans, Dravidians, Mongolians and Scythians. All these stocks of people came into India from various directions and with various cultures, centuries ago, when they were in a tribal state. They all in turn elbowed their entry into the country by fighting with their predecessors, and after a stomachful of it settled down as peaceful neighbours. Through constant contact and mutual intercourse they evolved a common culture that superseded their distinctive cultures. It may be granted that there has not been a thorough amalgamation of the various stocks that make up the peoples of India, and to a traveller from within the boundaries of India the East presents a marked contrast in physique and even in colour to the West, as does the South to the North. But amalgamation can never be the sole criterion of homogeneity as predicated of any people. Ethnically all people are heterogeneous. It is the unity of culture that is the basis of homogeneity. Taking this for granted, I venture to say that there is no country that can rival the Indian Peninsula with respect to the unity of its culture. It has not only a geographic unity, but it has over and above all a deeper and a much more fundamental unity—the indubitable cultural unity that covers the land from end to end. But it is because of this homogeneity that Caste becomes a problem so difficult to be explained. If the Hindu Society were a mere federation of mutually exclusive units, the matter would be simple enough. But Caste is a parcelling of an already homogeneous unit, and the explanation of the genesis of Caste is the explanation of this process of parcelling.

Before launching into our field of enquiry, it is better to advise ourselves regarding the nature of a caste I will therefore draw upon a few of the best students of caste for their definitions of it:

(1) Mr. Senart, a French authority, defines a caste as "a close corporation, in theory at any rate rigorously hereditary : equipped with a certain traditional and independent organisation, including a chief and a council, meeting on occasion in assemblies of more or less plenary

---

1. Ketkar, *Caste,* p. 4.

authority and joining together at certain festivals : bound together by common occupations, which relate more particularly to marriage and to food and to questions of ceremonial pollution, and ruling its members by the exercise of jurisdiction, the extent of which varies, but which succeeds in making the authority of the community more felt by the sanction of certain penalties and, above all, by final irrevocable exclusion from the group".

(2) Mr. Nesfield defines a caste as "a class of the community which disowns any connection with any other class and can neither intermarry nor eat nor drink with any but persons of their own community".

(3) According to Sir H. Risley, "a caste may be defined as a collection of families or groups of families bearing a common name which usually denotes or is associated with specific occupation, claiming common descent from a mythical ancestor, human or divine, professing to follow the same professional callings and are regarded by those who are competent to give an opinion as forming a single homogeneous community".

(4) Dr. Ketkar defines caste as "a social group having two characteristics : (i) membership is confined to those who are born of members and includes all persons so born ; (ii) the members are forbidden by an inexorable social law to marry outside the group".

To review these definitions is of great importance for our purpose. It will be noticed that taken individually the definitions of three of the writers include too much or too little : none is complete or correct by itself and all have missed the central point in the mechanism of the Caste system. Their mistake lies in trying to define caste as an isolated unit by itself, and not as a group within, and with definite relations to, the system of caste as a whole. Yet collectively all of them are complementary to one another, each one emphasising what has been obscured in the other. By way of criticism, therefore, I will take only those points common to all Castes in each of the above definitions which are regarded as peculiarities of Caste and evaluate them as such.

To start with Mr. Senart. He draws attention to the "idea of pollution" as a characteristic of Caste. With regard to this point it may be safely said that it is by no means a peculiarity of Caste as such. It usually originates in priestly ceremonialism and is a particular case of the general belief in purity. Consequently its necessary connection with Caste may be completely denied without damaging the working of Caste. The "idea of pollution" has been attached to the institution of Caste, only because the Caste that enjoys the highest rank is the priestly Caste : while we know that priest and purity are old associates. We may therefore conclude that the "idea of pollution" is a characteristic of Caste only in so far as Caste has a religious flavour.

Mr. Nesfield in his way dwells on the absence of messing with those outside the Caste as one of its characteristics. In spite of the newness of the point we must say that Mr. Nesfield has mistaken the effect for the cause. Caste, being a self-enclosed unit naturally limits social intercourse, including messing etc. to members within it. Consequently this absence of messing with outsiders is not due to positive prohibition, but is a natural result of Caste, *i.e.* exclusiveness. No doubt this absence of messing originally due to exclusiveness, acquired the prohibitory character of a religious injunction, but it may be regarded as a later growth. Sir H. Risley, makes no new point deserving of special attention.

We now pass on to the definition of Dr. Ketkar who has done much for the elucidation of the subject. Not only is he a native, but he has also brought a critical acumen and an open mind to bear on his study of Caste. His definition merits consideration, for he has defined Caste in its relation to a system of Castes, and has concentrated his attention only on those characteristics which are absolutely necessary for the existence of a Caste within a system, rightly excluding all others as being secondary or derivative in character. With respect to his definition it must, however, be said that in it there is a slight confusion of thought, lucid and clear as otherwise it is. He speaks of *Prohibition of Intermarriage* and *Membership by Autogeny* as the two characteristics of Caste. I submit that these are but two aspects of one and the same thing, and not two different things as Dr. Ketkar supposes them to be. If you prohibit intermarriage the result is that you limit membership to those born within the group. Thus the two are the obverse and the reverse sides of the same medal.

This critical evaluation of the various characteristics of Caste leave no doubt that prohibition, or rather the absence of intermarriage—endogamy, to be concise—is the only one that can be called the essence of Caste when rightly understood. But some may deny this on abstract anthropological grounds, for there exist endogamous groups without giving rise to the problem of Caste. In a general way this may be true, as endogamous societies, culturally different, making their abode in localities more or less removed, and having little to do with each other are a physical reality. The Negroes and the Whites and the various tribal groups that go by name of American Indians in the United States may be cited as more or less appropriate illustrations in support of this view. But we must not confuse matters, for in India the situation is different. As pointed out before, the peoples of India form a homogeneous whole. The various races of India occupying definite territories have more or less fused into one another and do possess cultural unity, which is the only criterion of a homogeneous population. Given this homogeneity as a basis, Caste becomes a problem altogether new in character and wholly absent in the situation constituted by the mere propinquity of endogamous social or tribal groups. Caste in India means an artificial chopping off of the population into fixed and definite units, each one prevented from fusing into another through the custom of endogamy. Thus the conclusion is inevitable that *Endogamy is the only characteristic that is peculiar to caste,* and if we succeed in showing how endogamy is maintained, we shall practically have proved the genesis and also the mechanism of Caste.

It may not be quite easy for you to anticipate why I regard endogamy as a key to the mystery of the Caste system. Not to strain your imagination too much, I will proceed to give you my reasons for it.

It may not also be out of place to emphasize at this moment that no civilized society of today presents more survivals of primitive times than does the Indian society. Its religion is essentially primitive and its tribal code, in spite of the advance of time and civilization, operates in all its pristine vigour even today. One of these primitive survivals, to which I wish particularly to draw your attention is the *Custom of Exogamy.* The prevalence of exogamy in the primitive worlds is a fact too wellknown to need any explanation. With the growth of history, however, exogamy has lost its efficacy, and excepting the nearest blood-kins, there is usually no social bar restricting the field of marriage. But regarding the peoples of India the law of exogamy is a positive injunction even today. Indian society still savours of the clan system, even though there are no clans; and this can be easily seen from the law of matrimony which centres round the principle of exogamy, for it is not that *Sapindas* (blood-kins) cannot marry, but a marriage even between *Sagotras* (of the same class) is regarded as a sacrilege.

Nothing is therefore more important for you to remember than the fact that endogamy is foreign to the people of India. The various *Gotras* of India are and have been exogamous : so are the other groups with totemic organization. It is no exaggeration to say that with the people of India exogamy is a creed and none dare infringe it, so much so that, in spite of the endogamy of the Castes within them, exogamy is strictly observed and that there are more rigorous penalties for violating exogamy than there are for violating endogamy. You will, therefore, readily see that with exogamy as the rule there could be no Caste, for exogamy means fusion. But we have castes ; consequently in the final analysis creation of Castes, so far as India is concerned, means the superposition of endogamy on exogamy. However, in an originally exogamous population an easy working out of endogamy (which is equivalent to the creation of Caste) is a grave problem, and it is in the consideration of the means utilized for the preservation of endogamy against exogamy that we may hope to find the solution of our problem.

*Thus the superposition of endogamy on exogamy means the creation of caste.* But this is not an easy affair. Let us take an imaginary group that desires to make itself into a Caste and analyse what means it will have to adopt to make itself endogamous. If a group desires to make itself endogamous a formal injunction against intermarriage with outside groups will be of no avail, especially if prior to the introduction of endogamy, exogamy had been the rule in all matrimonial relations. Again, there is a tendency in all groups lying in close contact with one another to assimilate and amalgamate, and thus consolidate into a homogeneous society. If this tendency is to be strongly counteracted in the interest of Caste formation, it is absolutely necessary to circumscribe a circle outside which people should not contract marriages.

Nevertheless, this encircling to prevent marriages from without creates problems from within which are not very easy of solution. Roughly speaking, in a normal group the two sexes are more or less evenly distributed, and generally speaking there is an equality between those of the same age. The equality is, however, never quite realized in actual societies. At the same time to the group that is desirous of making itself into a caste the maintenance of equality between the sexes becomes the ultimate goal, for without it. endogamy can no longer subsist. In other words, if endogamy is to be preserved conjugal rights from within have to be provided for, otherwise members of the group will be driven out of the circle to take care of themselves in any way they can. But in order that the conjugal rights be provided for from within, it is absolutely necessary to maintain a numerical equality between the marriageable units of the two sexes within the group desirous of making itself into a Caste. It is only through the maintenance of such an equality that the necessary endogamy of the group can be kept intact, and a very large disparity is sure to break it.

*The problem of Caste, then, ultimately resolves itself into one of repairing the disparity between the marriageable units of the two sexes within it.* Left to nature, the much needed parity between the units can be realized only when a couple dies simultaneously. But this is a rare contingency. The husband may die before the wife and create a *surplus woman,* who must be disposed of, else through intermarriage she will violate the endogamy of the group. In like manner the husband may survive his wife and be *surplus man,* whom the group, while it may sympathise with him for the sad bereavement, has to dispose of, else he will marry outside the Caste and will break the endogamy. Thus both the *surplus man* and the *surplus woman* constitute a menace to the Caste if not taken care of, for not finding suitable partners inside their prescribed circle (and left to themselves they cannot find any, for if the matter be not regulated there can only be just enough pairs to go round) very likely they will transgress the boundary, marry outside and import offspring that is foreign to the Caste.

Let us see what our imaginary group is likely to do with this *surplus man* and *surplus woman*. We will first take up the case of the *surplus woman*.

She can be disposed of in two different ways so as to preserve the endogamy of the Caste.

First: burn her on the funeral pyre of her deceased husband and get rid of her. This, however, is rather an impracticable way of solving the problem of sex disparity. In some cases it may work, in others it may not. Consequently every surplus woman cannot thus be disposed of, because it is an easy solution but a hard realization. And so the *surplus woman* (= widow), if not disposed of, remains in the group : but in her very existence lies a double danger. She may marry outside the Caste and violate endogamy, or she may marry within the Caste and through competition encroach upon the chances of marriage that must be reserved for the potential brides in the Caste. She is therefore a menace in any case, and something must be done to her if she cannot be burned along with her deceased husband.

The second remedy is to enforce widowhood on her for the rest of her life. So far as the objective results are concerned, burning is a better solution than enforcing widowhood. Burning the widow eliminates all the three evils that a *surplus woman* is fraught with. Being dead and gone she creates no problem of remarriage either inside or outside the Caste. But compulsory widowhood is superior to burning because it is more practicable. Besides being comparatively humane it also guards against the evils of remarriage as does burning; but it fails to guard the morals of the group. No doubt under compulsory widowhood the woman remains, and just because she is deprived of her natural right of being a legitimate wife in future, the incentive to immoral conduct is increased. But this is by no means an insuperable difficulty. She can be degraded to a condition in which she is no longer a source of allurement.

The problem of *surplus man* (= widower) is much more important and much more difficult than that of the *surplus woman* in a group that desires to make itself into a Caste. From time immemorial man as compared with woman has had the upper hand. He is a dominant figure in every group and of the two sexes has greater prestige. With this traditional superiority of man over woman his wishes have always been consulted. Woman, on the other hand, has been an easy prey to all kinds of iniquitous injunctions, religious, social or economic. But man as a maker of injunctions is most often above them all. Such being the case, you cannot accord the same kind of treatment to a *surplus man* as you can to a *surplus woman* in a Caste.

The project of burning him with his deceased wife is hazardous in two ways : first of all it cannot be done, simply because he is a man. Secondly, if done, a sturdy soul is lost to the Caste. There remain then only two solutions which can conveniently dispose of him. I say conveniently, because he is an asset to the group.

Important as he is to the group, endogamy is still more important, and the solution must assure both these ends. Under these circumstances he may be forced or I should say induced, after the manner of the widow, to remain a widower for the rest of his life. This solution is not altogether difficult, for without any compulsion some are so disposed as to enjoy self-imposed celibacy, or even to take a further step of their own accord and renounce the world and its joys. But, given human nature as it is, this solution can hardly be expected to be realized. On the other hand, as is very likely to be the case, if the *surplus man* remains in the group as an active participator in group activities, he is a danger to the morals of the group. Looked at from a different point of view celibacy, though easy in cases where it succeeds, is not so advantageous even then to the material prospects of the Caste. If he observes genuine celibacy and renounces the world, he would not be a menace to the preservation of Caste endogamy or Caste morals as he undoubtedly would be if he remained a secular person. But as an ascetic celibate he is as good as burned, so far as the material well-being of his Caste is concerned. A Caste, in order that it may be large enough to afford a vigorous communal life, must be maintained at a certain numerical strength. But to hope for this and to proclaim celibacy is the same as trying to cure atrophy by bleeding.

Imposing celibacy on the *surplus man* in the group, therefore, fails both theoretically and practically. It is in the interest of the Caste to keep him as a *Grahastha* (one who raises a family), to use a Sanskrit technical term. But the problem is to provide him with a wife from within the Caste. At the outset this is not possible, for the ruling ratio in a caste has to be one man to one woman and none can have two chances of marriage, for in a Caste thoroughly self-enclosed there are always just enough marriageable women to go round for the marriageable men. Under these circumstances the *surplus man* can be provided with a wife only by recruiting a bride from the ranks of those not yet marriageable in order to tie him down to the group. This is certainly the best of the possible solutions in the case of the *surplus man*. By this, he is kept within the Caste. By this means numerical depletion through constant outflow is guarded against, and by this endogamy morals are preserved.

It will now be seen that the four means by which numerical disparity between the two sexes is conveniently maintained are : (1) burning the widow with her deceased husband ; (2) compulsory widowhood—a milder form of burning ; (3) imposing celibacy on the widower and (4) wedding him to a girl not yet marriageable. Though, as I said above, burning the widow and imposing celibacy on the widower are of doubtful service to the group in its endeavour to preserve its endogamy, all of them operate as *means*. But means, as forces, when liberated or set in motion create an end. What then is the end that these means create ? They create and perpetuate endogamy, while caste and endogamy, according to our analysis of the various definitions of caste, are one and the same thing. Thus the existence of these means is identical with caste and caste involves these means.

This, in my opinion, is the general mechanism of a caste in a system of castes. Let us now turn from these high generalities to the castes in Hindu Society and inquire into their mechanism. I need hardly premise that there are a great many pitfalls in the path of those who try to unfold the past, and caste in India to be sure is a very ancient institution. This is especially true where there exist no authentic or written records or where the people, like the Hindus, are so constituted that to them writing history is a folly, for the world is an illusion. But institutions do live, though for a long time they may remain unrecorded and as often as not customs and morals are like fossils that tell their own history. If this is true, our task will be amply rewarded if we scrutinize the solution the Hindus arrived at to meet the problems of the *surplus man* and *surplus woman*.

Complex though it be in its general working the Hindu Society, even to a superficial observer, presents three singular uxorial customs, namely :

(i) *Sati* or the burning of the widow on the funeral pyre of her deceased husband.

(ii) Enforced widowhood by which a widow is not allowed to remarry.

(iii) Girl marriage.

In addition, one also notes a great hankering after *Sannyasa* (renunciation) on the part of the widower, but this may in some cases be due purely to psychic disposition.

So far as I know, no scientific explanation of the origin of these customs is forthcoming even today. We have plenty of philosophy to tell us why these customs were honoured, but nothing to tell us the causes of their origin and existence. *Sati* has been honoured (*Cf.* A. K. Coomaraswamy, *Sati:* A Defence of the Eastern Woman in the British Sociological Review, Vol. VI, 1913) because it is a "proof of the perfect unity of body and soul" between husband and wife and of "devotion beyond the grave", because it embodied the ideal of wifehood, which is well expressed by Uma when she said, "Devotion to her Lord is woman's honour, it is her eternal heaven : and O Maheshvara", she adds with a most touching human cry, "I desire not paradise itself if thou are not satisfied with me !" Why compulsory widowhood is honoured I know not, nor have I yet met with any one who sang in praise of it, though there are a great many who adhere to it. The eulogy in honour of girl marriage is reported by Dr. Ketkar to be as follows : "A really faithful man or woman ought not to feel affection for a woman or a man other than the one with whom he or she is united. Such purity is compulsory not only after marriage, but even before marriage, for that is the only correct ideal of chastity. No maiden could be considered pure if she feels love for a man other than the one to whom she might be married. As she does not know to whom she is going to be married, she must not feel affection for any man at all before marriage. If she does so, it is a sin. So it is better for a girl to know whom she has to love before any sexual consciousness has been awakened in her."[2] Hence girl marriage.

This high-flown and ingenious sophistry indicates why these institutions were honoured, but does not tell us why they were practised. My own interpretation is that they were honoured because they were practised. Any one slightly acquainted with rise of individualism in the 18th century will appreciate my remark. At all times, it is the movement that is most important; and the philosophies grow around it long afterwards to justify it and give it a moral support. In like manner I urge that the very fact that these customs were so highly eulogized proves that they needed eulogy for their prevalence. Regarding the question as to why they arose, I submit that they were needed to create the structure of caste and the philosophies in honour of them were intended to popularize them, or to gild the pill, as we might say, for they must have been so abominable and shocking to the moral sense of the unsophisticated that they needed a great deal of sweetening. These customs are essentially of the nature of *means,* though they are represented as ideals. But this should not blind us from understanding the *results* that flow from them. One might safely say that idealization of means is necessary and in this particular case was perhaps motivated to endow them with greater efficacy. Calling a means an end does no harm, except that it disguises its real character; but it does not deprive it of its real nature, that of a means. You may pass a law that all cats are dogs, just as you can call a means an end. But you can no more change the nature of means thereby than you can turn cats into dogs; consequently I am justified in holding that, whether regarded as ends or as means, *Sati, enforced widowhood* and *girl marriage* are customs that were primarily intended to solve the problem of the *surplus man* and *surplus woman* in a caste and to maintain its endogamy. Strict endogamy could not be preserved without these customs, while caste without endogamy is a fake.

Having explained the mechanism of the creation and preservation of Caste in India, the further question as to its genesis naturally arises. The question or origin is always an annoying question and in the study of Caste it is sadly neglected; some have connived at it, while others have dodged it. Some are puzzled as to whether there could be such a thing as the origin of caste and suggest that "if we cannot control our fondness for the word 'origin', we should better use the plural form, viz. 'origins of caste' ". As for myself I do not feel puzzled by the Origin of Caste in India for, as I have established before, endogamy is the only characteristic of Caste and when I say *Origin of Caste* I mean *The Origin of the Mechanism for Endogamy.*

---

2. *History of Caste in India,* 1909, pp. 2-33.

The atomistic conception of individuals in a Society so greatly popularised—I was about to say vulgarized—in political orations is the greatest humbug. To say that individuals make up society is trivial; society is always composed of classes. It may be an exaggeration to assert the theory of class-conflict, but the existence of definite classes in a society is a fact. Their basis may differ. They may be economic or intellectual or social, but an individual in a society is always a member of a class. This is a universal fact and early Hindu society could not have been an exception to this rule, and, as a matter of fact, we know it was not. If we bear this generalization in mind, our study of the genesis of caste would be very much facilitated, for we have only to determine what was the class that first made itself into a caste, for class and caste, so to say, are next door neighbours, and it is only a span that separates the two. *A Caste is an Enclosed Class.*

The study of the origin of caste must furnish us with an answer to the question—what is the class that raised this "enclosure" around itself? The question may seem too inquisitorial, but it is pertinent, and an answer to this will serve us to elucidate the mystery of the growth and development of castes all over India. Unfortunately a direct answer to this question is not within my power. I can answer it only indirectly. I said just above that the customs in question were current in the Hindu society. To be true to facts it is necessary to qualify the statement, as it connotes universality of their prevalence. These customs in all their strictness are obtainable only in one caste, namely the Brahmins, who occupy the highest place in the social hierarchy of the Hindu society; and as their prevalence in non-Brahmin castes is derivative of their observance is neither strict nor complete. This important fact can serve as a basis of an important observation. If the prevalence of these customs in the non-Brahmin Castes is derivative, as can be shown very easily, then it needs no argument to prove what class is the father of the institution of caste. Why the Brahmin class should have enclosed itself into a caste is a different question, which may be left as an employment for another occasion. But the strict observance of these customs and the social superiority arrogated by the priestly class in all ancient civilizations are sufficient to prove that they were the originators of this "unnatural institution" founded and maintained through those unnatural means.

I now come to the third part of my paper regarding the question of the growth and spread of the caste system all over India. The question I have to answer is: How did the institution of caste spread among the rest of the non-Brahmin population of the country? The question of the spread of the castes all over India has suffered a worse fate than the question of genesis. And the main cause, as it seems to me, is that the two questions of spread and of origin are not separated. This is because of the common belief among scholars that the caste system has either been imposed upon the docile population of India by a law-giver as a divine dispensation, or that it has grown according to some law of social growth peculiar to the Indian people.

I first propose to handle the law-giver of India. Every country has its law-giver, who arises as an incarnation *(avatar)* in times of emergency to set right a sinning humanity and give it the laws of justice and morality. Manu, the law-giver of India, if he did exist, was certainly an audacious person. If the story that he gave the law of caste be credited, then Manu must have been a dare-devil fellow and the humanity that accepted his dispensation must be a humanity quite different from the one we are acquainted with. It is unimaginable that the law of caste was *given*. It is hardly an exaggeration to say that Manu could not have outlived his law, for what is that class that can submit to be degraded to the status of brutes by the pen of a man, and suffer him to raise another class to the pinnacle? Unless he was a tyrant who held all the population in subjection it cannot be imagined that he could have been allowed to dispense his patronage in this grossly unjust manner, as may be easily seen by a mere glance at his "Institutes". I may seem hard on Manu. but I am sure my force is not strong enough to kill his ghost. He lives, like a disembodied spirit and is appealed to, and I am afraid will yet live long. One thing I want to impress upon you is that Manu did not *give the law* of Caste and that he could not do so. Caste existed long before Manu. He was an upholder of it and therefore philosophised about it, but certainly he did not and could not ordain the present order of Hindu Society. His work ended with the codification of existing caste rules and the preaching of Caste *Dharma*. The spread and growth of the Caste system is too gigantic a task to be achieved by the power or cunning of an individual or of a class. Similar in argument is the theory that the Brahmins created the Caste. After what I have said regarding Manu, I need hardly say anything more, except to point out that it is incorrect in thought and malicious in intent. The Brahmins may have been guilty of many things, and I dare say they were, but the imposing of the caste system on the non-Brahmin population was beyond their mettle. They may have helped the process by their glib philosophy, but they certainly could not have pushed their scheme beyond their own confines. To fashion society after one's own pattern! How glorious! How hard! One can take pleasure and eulogize its furtherance, but cannot further it very far. The vehemence of my attack may seem to be unnecessary; but I can assure you that it is not uncalled for. There is a strong belief in the mind of orthodox Hindus that the Hindu Society was somehow moulded into the framework of the Caste System and that it is an organization consciously created by the *Shastras*. Not only does this belief exist, but it is being justified on the ground that it cannot but be good, because it is ordained by the *Shastras* and the *Shastras* cannot be wrong. I have urged so much on the adverse side of this attitude, not because the religious sanctity is grounded on scientific basis, nor to help those reformers who are preaching against it. Preaching did not make the caste system neither will it unmake it. My aim is to show the falsity of the attitude that has exalted religious sanction to the position of a scientific explanation.

Thus the great man theory does not help us very far in solving the spread of castes in India. Western scholars, probably not much given to hero-worship, have attempted other explanations. The nuclei, round which have "formed" the various castes in India, are, according to them : (1) occupation; (2) survivals of tribal organizations etc. ; (3) the rise of new belief; (4) cross-breeding and (5) migration.

The question may be asked whether these nuclei do not exist in other societies and whether they are peculiar to India. If they are not peculiar to India, but are common to the world, why is it that they did not "form" caste on other parts of this planet ? Is it because those parts are holier than the land of the *Vedas,* or that the professors are mistaken ? I am afraid that the latter is the truth.

In spite of the high theoretic value claimed by the several authors for their respective theories based on one or other of the above nuclei, one regrets to say that on close examination they are nothing more than filling illustrations— what Matthew Arnold means by "the grand name without the grand thing in it". Such are the various theories of caste advanced by Sir Denzil Ibbetson, Mr. Nesfield, Mr. Senart and Sir H. Risley. To criticise them in a lump would be to say that they are a disguised form of the *Petitio Principii* of formal logic. To illustrate : Mr. Nesfield says that "function and function only. .. was the foundation upon which the whole system of Castes in India was built up". But he may rightly be reminded that he does not very much advance our thought by making the above statement, which practically amounts to saying that castes in India are functional or occupational, which is a very poor discovery ! We have yet to know from Mr. Nesfield why is it that an occupational group turned into an occupational caste ? I would very cheerfully have undertaken the task of dwelling on the theories of other ethnologists, had it not been for the fact that Mr. Nesfield's is a typical one.

Without stopping to criticize those theories that explain the caste system as a natural phenomenon occurring in obedience to the law of disintegration, as explained by Herbert Spencer in his formula of evolution, or as natural as "the structural differentiation within an organism"—to employ the phraseology of orthodox apologists—, or as an early attempt to test the laws of eugenics—as all belonging to the same class of fallacy which regards the caste system as inevitable, or as being consciously imposed in anticipation of these laws on a helpless and humble population, I will now lay before you my own view on the subject.

We shall be well advised to recall at the outset that the Hindu society, in common with other societies, was composed of classes and the earliest known are the (1) Brahmins or the priestly class; (2) the Kshatriya, or the military class; (3) the Vaishya, or the merchant class and (4) the Shudra, or the artisan and menial class. Particular attention has to be paid to the fact that this was essentially a class system, in which individuals, when qualified, could change their class, and therefore classes did change their personnel. At some time in the history of the Hindus, the priestly class socially detached itself from the rest of the body of people and through a closed-door policy became a caste by itself. The other classes being subject to the law of social division of labour underwent differentiation, some into large, others into very minute groups. The Vaishya and Shudra classes were the original inchoate plasm, which formed the sources of the numerous castes of today. As the military occupation does not very easily lend itself to very minute sub-division, the Kshatriya class could have differentiated into soldiers and administrators.

This sub-division of a society is quite natural. But the unnatural thing about these sub-divisions is that they have lost the open-door character of the class system and have become self-enclosed units called castes. The question is: were they compelled to close their doors and become endogamous, or did they close them of their own accord? I submit that there is a double line of answer: *Some closed the door: Others found it closed against them.* The one is a psychological interpretation and the other is mechanistic, but they are complementary and both are necessary to explain the phenomena of caste-formation in its entirety.

I will first take up the psychological interpretation. The question we have to answer in this connection is: Why did these sub-divisions or classes, if you please, industrial, religious or otherwise, become self-enclosed or endogamous? My answer is because the Brahmins were so. Endogamy or the closed-door system, was a fashion in the Hindu society, and as it had originated from the Brahmin caste it was whole-heartedly imitated by all the non-Brahmin sub-divisions or classes, who, in their turn, became endogamous castes. It is "the infection of imitation" that caught all these sub-divisions on their onward march of differentiation and has turned them into castes. The propensity to imitate is a deep-seated one in the human mind and need not be deemed an inadequate explanation for the formation of the various castes in India. It is so deep-seated that Walter Bagehot argues that, "We must not think of . . . imitation as voluntary, or even conscious. On the contrary it has its seat mainly in very obscure parts of the mind, whose notions, so far from being consciously produced, are hardly felt to exist; so far from being conceived beforehand, are not even felt at the time. The main seat of the imitative part of our nature is our belief, and the causes predisposing us to believe this or disinclining us to believe that are among the obscurest parts of our nature. But as to the imitative nature of credulity there can be no doubt."[3] This propensity to imitate has been made the subject of a scientific study by Gabriel Tarde, who lays down three laws of imitation. One of his three laws is that imitation flows from the higher to the lower or, to quote his own words, "Given the opportunity, a nobility will always and everywhere imitate its leaders, its kings or sovereigns, and the people likewise, given the opportunity, its nobility."[4] Another of Tarde's laws of imitation is : that the extent or intensity of imitation varies inversely in proportion to distance, or in his own words "The thing that is most imitated is the most superior one of those that are nearest. In fact, the influence of the model's example is efficacious inversely to its *distance* as well as directly to its superiority. Distance is understood here in its sociological meaning. However distant in space a stranger may be, he is close by, from this point of view, if we have numerous and daily relations with him and if we have every facility to satisfy our desire to imitate him. This law of the imitation of the nearest, of the least distant, explains the gradual and consecutive character of the spread of an example that has been set by the higher social ranks."[5]

In order to prove my thesis—which really needs no proof—that some castes were formed by imitation, the best way, it seems to me, is to find out whether or not the vital conditions for the formation of castes by imitation exist in the Hindu Society. The conditions for imitation, according to this standard authority are : (1) that the source of imitation must enjoy prestige in the group and (2) that there must be "numerous and daily relations" among members of a group. That these conditions were present in India there is little reason to doubt. The Brahmin is a semi-god and very nearly a demi-god. He sets up a mode and moulds the rest. His prestige is unquestionable and is the fountain-head of bliss and good. Can such a being, idolised by scriptures and venerated by the priest-ridden multitude, fail to project his personality on the suppliant humanity ? Why, if the story be true, he is believed to be the very end of creation. Such a creature is worthy of more than mere imitation, but at least of imitation ; and if he lives in an endogamous enclosure, should not the rest follow his example ? Frail humanity! Be it embodied in a grave philosopher or a frivolous housemaid, it succumbs. It cannot be otherwise. Imitation is easy and invention is difficult.

Yet another way of demonstrating the play of imitation in the formation of castes is to understand the attitude of non-Brahmin classes towards those customs which supported the structure of caste in its nascent days until, in the course of history, it became embedded in the Hindu mind and hangs there to this day without any support—for now it needs no prop but belief—like

---

3. *Physics and Politics,* 1915, p. 60.
4. *Laws of Imitation,* Tr. by E.C. Parsons, 2nd edition, p. 217.
5. *Ibid.,* p. 224.

a weed on the surface of a pond. In a way, but only in a way, the status of a caste in the Hindu Society varies directly with the extent of the observance of the customs of *Sati,* enforced widowhood, and girl marriage. But observance of these customs varies directly with the *distance* (I am using the word in the Tardian sense) that separates the caste. Those castes that are nearest to the Brahmins have imitated all the three customs and insist on the strict observance thereof. Those that are less near have imitated enforced widowhood and girl marriage; others, a little further off, have only girl marriage and those furthest off have imitated only the belief in the caste principle. This imperfect imitation, I dare say, is due partly to what Tarde calls "distance" and partly to the barbarous character of these customs. This phenomenon is a complete illustration of Tarde's law and leaves no doubt that the whole process of caste-formation in India is a process of imitation of the higher by the lower. At this juncture I will turn back to support a former conclusion of mine, which might have appeared to you as too sudden or unsupported. I said that the Brahmin class first raised the structure of caste by the help of those three customs in question. My reason for that conclusion was that their existence in other classes was derivative. After what I have said regarding the role of imitation in the spread of these customs among the non-Brahmin castes, as means or as ideals, though the imitators have not been aware of it, they exist among them as derivatives; and, if they are derived, there must have been prevalent one original caste that was high enough to have served as a pattern for the rest. But in a theocratic society, who could be the pattern but the servant of God?

This completes the story of those that were weak enough to close their doors. Let us now see how others were closed in as a result of being closed out. This I call the mechanistic process of the formation of caste. It is mechanistic because it is inevitable. That this line of approach, as well as the psychological one, to the explanation of the subject has escaped my predecessors is entirely due to the fact that they have conceived caste as a unit by itself and not as one within a System of Caste. The result of this oversight or lack of sight has been very detrimental to the proper understanding of the subject matter and therefore its correct explanation. I will proceed to offer my own explanation by making one remark which I will urge you to bear constantly in mind. It is this: that *caste in the singular number is an unreality. Castes exist only in the plural number.* There is no such thing as a caste: There are always castes. To illustrate my meaning: while making themselves into a caste, the Brahmins, by virtue of this, created non-Brahmin caste; or, to express it in my own way, while closing themselves in they closed others out. I will clear my point by taking another illustration. Take India as a whole with its various communities designated by the various creeds to which they owe allegiance, to wit, the Hindus, Mohammedans, Jews, Christians and Parsis. Now, barring the Hindus, the rest within themselves are non-caste communities.

But with respect to each other they are castes. Again, if the first four enclose themselves, the Parsis are directly closed out, but are indirectly closed in. Symbolically, if Group A wants to be endogamous, Group B has to be so by sheer force of circumstances.

Now apply the same logic to the Hindu society and you have another explanation of the "fissiparous" character of caste, as a consequence of the virtue of self-duplication that is inherent in it. Any innovation that seriously antagonises the ethical, religious and social code of the Caste is not likely to be tolerated by the Caste, and the recalcitrant members of a Caste are in danger of being thrown out of the Caste, and left to their own fate without having the alternative of being admitted into or absorbed by other Castes. Caste rules are inexorable and they do not wait to make nice distinctions between kinds of offence. Innovation may be of any kind, but all kinds will suffer the same penalty. A novel way of thinking will create a new Caste for the old ones will not tolerate it. The noxious thinker respectfully called Guru (Prophet) suffers the same fate as the sinners in illegitimate love. The former creates a caste of the nature of a religious sect and the latter a type of mixed caste. Castes have no mercy for a sinner who has the courage to violate the code. The penalty is excommunication and the result is a new caste. It is not peculiar Hindu psychology that induces the excommunicated to form themselves into a caste; far from it. On the contrary, very often they have been quite willing to be humble members of some caste (higher by preference) if they could be admitted within its fold. But castes are enclosed units and it is their conspiracy with clear conscience that compels the excommunicated to make themselves into a caste. The logic of this obdurate circumstance is merciless, and it is in obedience to its force that some unfortunate groups find themselves enclosed, because others in enclosing, themselves have closed them out, with the result that new groups (formed on any basis obnoxious to the caste rules) by a mechanical law are constantly being converted into castes to a bewildering multiplicity. Thus is told the second tale in the process of Caste formation in India.

Now to summarise the main points of my thesis. In my opinion there have been several mistakes committed by the students of Caste, which have misled them in their investigations. European students of Caste have unduly emphasised the role of colour in the Caste system. Themselves impregnated by colour prejudices, they very readily imagined it to be the chief factor in the Caste problem. But nothing can be farther from the truth, and Dr. Ketkar is correct when he insists that "All the princes whether they belonged to the so-called Aryan race, or the so-called Dravidian race, were Aryas. Whether a tribe or a family was racially Aryan or Dravidian was a question which never troubled the people of India, until foreign scholars came in and began to draw the line. The colour of the skin had long ceased to be a matter of importance."[6] Again, they have mistaken mere descriptions for explanation and fought over them as though they were theories of origin. There are occupational, religious etc., castes, it is true, but it is by no means an explanation of the origin of Caste. We have yet to find out why occupational groups are castes; but this question has never even been raised. Lastly they have taken Caste very lightly as though a breath had made it. On the contrary, Caste, as I have explained it, is almost impossible to be sustained : for the difficulties that it involves are tremendous. It is true that Caste rests on belief, but before belief comes to be the foundation of an institution, the institution itself needs to be perpetuated and fortified. My study of the Caste problem involves four main points : (1) that in spite of the composite make-up of the Hindu population, there is a deep cultural unity; (2) that caste is a parcelling into bits of a larger cultural unit; (3) that there was one caste to start with and (4) that classes have become Castes through imitation and excommunication.

Peculiar interest attaches to the problem of Caste in India today; as persistent attempts are being made to do away with this unnatural institution. Such attempts at reform, however, have aroused a great deal of controversy regarding its origin, as to whether it is due to the conscious command of a Supreme Authority, or is an unconscious growth in the life of a human society under peculiar circumstances. Those who hold the latter view will, I hope, find some food for thought in the standpoint adopted in this paper. Apart from its practical importance the subject of Caste is an all absorbing problem and the interest aroused in me regarding its theoretic foundations has moved me to put before you some of the conclusions, which seem to me well founded, and the grounds upon which they may be supported. I am not, however, so presumptuous as to think them in any way final, or anything more than a contribution to a discussion of the subject. It seems to me that the car has been shunted on wrong lines, and the primary object of the paper is to indicate what I regard to be the right path of investigation, with a view to arrive at a serviceable truth. We must, however, guard against approaching the subject with a bias. Sentiment must be outlawed from the domain of science and things should be judged from an objective standpoint. For myself I shall find as much pleasure in a positive destruction of my own idealogy, as in a rational disagreement on a topic, which, notwithstanding many learned disquisitions is likely to remain controversial forever. To conclude, while I am ambitious to advance a Theory of Caste, if it can be shown to be untenable I shall be equally willing to give it up.

••

---

6. *History of Caste*, p. 82.

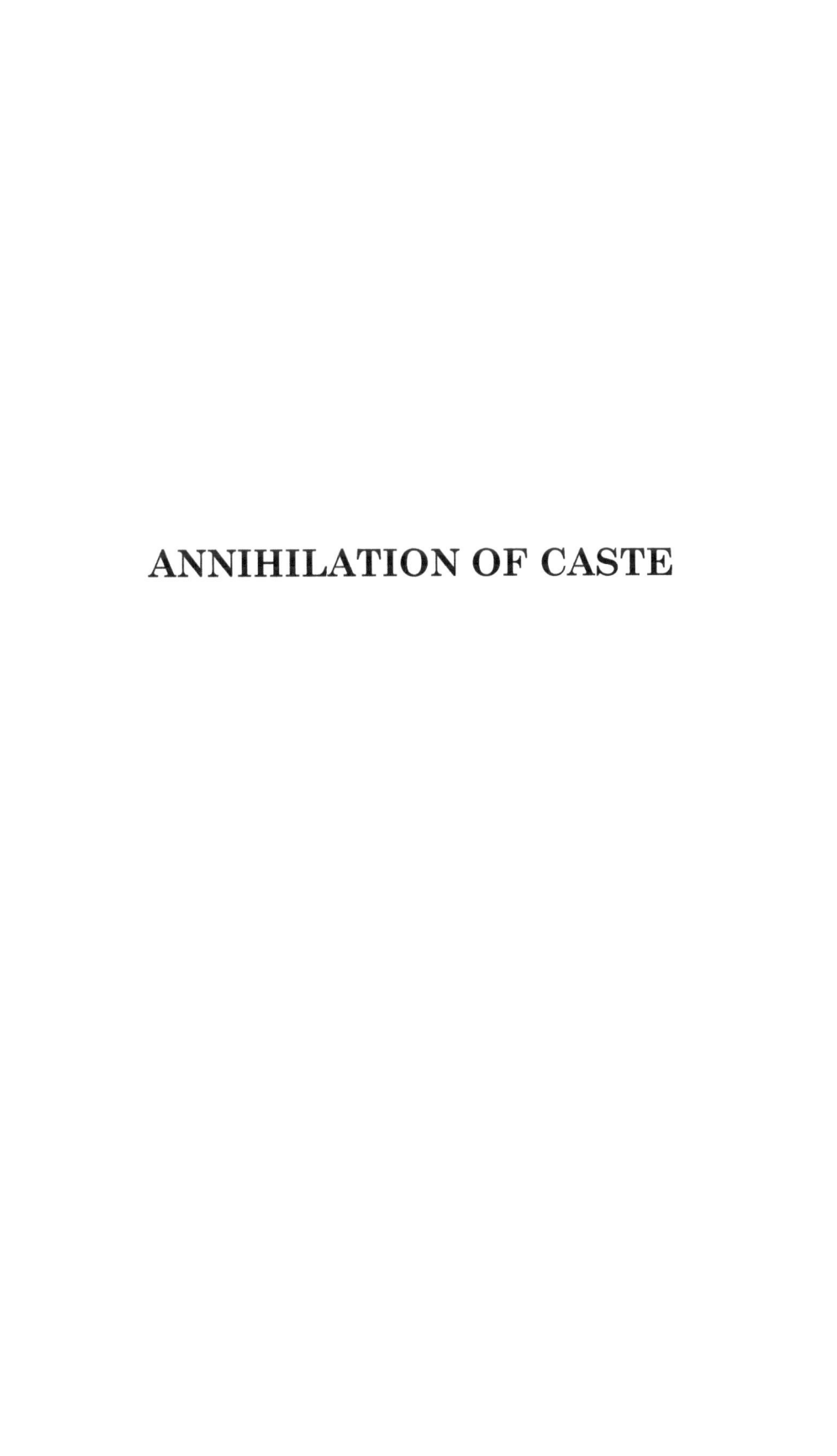

# ANNIHILATION OF CASTE

# ANNIHILATION OF CASTE

## PREFACE TO THE SECOND EDITION

The speech prepared by me for the Jat-Pat-Todak Mandal of Lahore has had an astonishingly warm reception from the Hindu public for whom it was primarily intended. The English edition of one thousand five hundred was exhausted within two months of its publication. It is translated into Gujarati and Tamil. It is being translated in Marathi, Hindi, Punjabi and Malayalam. The demand for the English text still continues unabated. To satisfy this demand it has become necessary to issue a Second Edition. Considerations of history and effectiveness of appeal have led me to retain the original form of the essay—namely the speech form—although I was asked to recast it in the form of a direct narrative. To this edition I have added two appendices. I have collected in Appendix I the two articles written by Mr. Gandhi by way of review of my speech in the *Harijan,* and his letter to Mr. Sant Ram, a member of the Jat-Pat-Todak Mandal. In Appendix II, I have printed my views in reply to the articles of Mr. Gandhi collected in Appendix I. Besides Mr. Gandhi many others have adversely criticised my views as expressed in my speech. But I have felt that in taking notice of such adverse comments I should limit myself to Mr. Gandhi. This I have done not because what he has said is so weighty as to deserve a reply but because to many a Hindu he is an oracle, so great that when he opens his lips it is expected that the argument must close and no dog must bark. But the world owes much to rebels who would dare to argue in the face of the pontiff and insist that he is not infallible. I do not care for the credit which every progressive society must give to its rebels. I shall be satisfied if I make the Hindus realize that they are the sick men of India and that their sickness is causing danger to the health and happiness of other Indians.

**B. R. AMBEDKAR**

## PREFACE TO THE THIRD EDITION

The Second edition of this Essay appeared in 1937, and was exhausted within a very short period. A new edition has been in demand for a long time. It was my intention to recast the essay so as to incorporate into it another essay of mine called *"Castes in India, their Origin and their Mechanism"*, which appeared in the issue of the Indian Antiquary Journal for May 1917. But as I could not find time, and as there is very little prospect of my being able to do so and as the demand for it from the public is very insistent, I am content to let this be a mere reprint of the Second edition.

I am glad to find that this essay has become so popular, and I hope that it will serve the purpose for which it was intended.

**22, Prithwiraj Road**  **B. R. AMBEDKAR**
**New Delhi**
**1st December 1944**

# PROLOGUE

On December 12, 1935, I received the following letter from Mr. Sant Ram, the Secretary of the Jat-Pat-Todak Mandal:

My dear Doctor Saheb,

Many thanks for your kind letter of the 5th December. I have released it for press without your permission for which I beg your pardon, as I saw no harm in giving it publicity. You are a great thinker, and it is my well-considered opinion that none else has studied the problem of Caste so deeply as you have. I have always benefited myself and our Mandal from your ideas. I have explained and preached it in the *Kranti* many times and I have even lectured on it in many Conferences. I am now very anxious to read the exposition of your new formula—"It is not possible to break Caste without annihilating the religious notions on which it, the Caste system, is founded." Please do explain it at length at your earliest convenience, so that we may take up the idea and emphasise it from press and platform. At present, it is not fully clear to me.

\*        \*        \*        \*        \*

Our Executive Committee persists in having you as our President for our Annual Conference. We can change our dates to accommodate your convenience. Independent Harijans of Punjab are very much desirous to meet you and discuss with you their plans. So if you kindly accept our request and come to Lahore to preside over the Conference it will serve double purpose. We will invite Harijan leaders of all shades of opinion and you will get an opportunity of giving your ideas to them.

The Mandal has deputed our Assistant Secretary, Mr. Indra Singh, to meet you at Bombay in Xmas and discuss with you the whole situation with a view to persuade you to please accept our request.

\*        \*        \*        \*        \*

The Jat-Pat-Todak Mandal, I was given to understand, to be an organization of Caste Hindu Social Reformers, with the one and only aim, namely to eradicate the Caste System from amongst the Hindus. As a rule, I do not like to take any part in a movement which is carried on by the Caste Hindus. Their attitude towards social reform is so different from mine that I have found it difficult to pull on with them. Indeed, I find their company quite uncongenial to me on account of our differences of opinion. Therefore when the Mandal first approached me I declined their invitation to preside. The Mandal, however, would not take a refusal from me and sent down one of its members to Bombay to press me to accept the invitation. In the end I agreed to preside. The Annual Conference was to be held at Lahore, the headquarters of the Mandal. The Conference was to meet in Easter but was subsequently postponed to the middle of May 1936. The Reception Committee of the Mandal has now cancelled the Conference. The notice of cancellation came long after my Presidential address had been printed. The copies of this address are now lying with me. As I did not get an opportunity to deliver the address from the presidential chair the public has not had an opportunity to know my views on the problems created by the Caste System. To let the public know them and also to dispose of the printed copies which are lying on my hand, I have decided to put the printed copies of the address in the market. The accompanying pages contain the text of that address.

The public will be curious to know what led to the cancellation of my appointment as the President of the Conference. At the start, a dispute arose over the printing of the address. I desired that the address should be printed in Bombay. The Mandal wished that it should be printed in Lahore on the ground of economy. I did not agree and insisted upon having it printed in Bombay. Instead of agreeing to my proposition I received a letter signed by several members of the Mandal from which I give the following extract:

27-3-36

Revered Dr. Ji,

Your letter of the 24th instant addressed to Sjt. Sant Ram has been shown to us. We were a little disappointed to read it. Perhaps you are not fully aware of the situation that has arisen here. Almost all the Hindus in the Punjab are against your being invited to this province. The Jat-Pat-Todak Mandal has been subjected to the bitterest criticism and has received censorious rebuke from all quarters. All the Hindu leaders among whom being Bhai Parmanand, ML.A. (Ex-President, Hindu Maha Sabha), Mahatma Hans Raj, Dr. Gokal Chand Narang, Minister for Local Self-Government, Raja Narendra Nath, M.L.C. etc., have dissociated themselves from this step of the Mandal.

Despite all this the runners of the Jat-Pat-Todak Mandal (the leading figure being Sjt. Sant Ram) are determined to wade through thick and thin but would not give up the idea of your presidentship. The Mandal has earned a bad name.

*　　　　　*　　　　　*　　　　　*　　　　　*

Under the circumstances it becomes your duty to co-operate with the Mandal. On the one hand, they are being put to so much trouble and hardship by the Hindus and if on the other hand you too augment their difficulties it will be a most sad coincidence of bad luck for them.

We hope you will think over the matter and do what is good for us all.

*　　　　　*　　　　　*　　　　　*　　　　　*

This letter puzzled me greatly. I could not understand why the Mandal should displease me for the sake of a few rupees in the matter of printing the address. Secondly, I could not believe that men like Sir Gokal Chand Narang had really resigned as a protest against my selection as President because I had received the following letter from Sir Gokal Chand himself:

5 Montgomery Road
Lahore, 7-2-36

Dear Doctor Ambedkar,

I am glad to learn from the workers of the Jat-Pat-Todak Mandal that you have agreed to preside at their next anniversary to be held at Lahore during the Easter holidays. It will give me much pleasure if you stay with me while you are at Lahore. More when we meet.

Yours sincerely,
G. C. NARANG

Whatever be the truth I did not yield to this pressure. But even when the Mandal found that I was insisting upon having my address printed in Bombay instead of agreeing to my proposal the Mandal sent me a wire that they were sending Mr. Har Bhagwan to Bombay to "talk over matters personally" Mr. Har Bhagwan came to Bombay on the 9th of April. When I met Mr. Har Bhagwan I found that he had nothing to say regarding the issue. Indeed, he was so unconcerned regarding the printing of the address, whether it should be printed in Bombay or in Lahore, that he did not even mention it in the course of our conversation. All that he was anxious for was to know the contents of the address. I was then convinced that in getting the address printed in Lahore the main object of the Mandal was not to save money but to get at the contents of the address. I gave him a copy. He did not feel very happy with some parts of it. He returned to Lahore. From Lahore, he wrote to me the following letter:

Lahore, dated April 14, 1936

My dear Doctor Sahib,

Since my arrival from Bombay, on the 12th, I have been indisposed owing to my having not slept continuously for 5 or 6 nights, which were spent in the train. Reaching here I came to know that you had come to Amritsar. I would have seen you there if I were well enough to go about. I have made over your address to Mr. Sant Ram for translation and he has liked it very much, but he is not sure whether it could be translated by him for printing before the 25th. In any case, it woud have a wide publicity and we are sure it would wake the Hindus up from their slumber.

The passage I pointed out to you at Bombay has been read by some of our friends with a little misgiving, and those of us who would like to see the Conference terminate without any untoward incident would prefer that at least the word "Veda" be left out for the time being. I leave this to your good sense. I hope, however, in your concluding paragraphs you will make it clear that the views expressed in the address are your own and that the responsibility does not lie on the Mandal. I hope, you will not mind this statement of mine and would let us have 1,000 copies of the address, for which we shall, of course, pay. To this effect I have sent you a telegram today. A cheque of Rs. 100 is enclosed herewith which kindly acknowledge, and send us your bills in due time.

I have called a meeting of the Reception Committee and shall communicate their decision to you immediately. In the meantime kindly accept my heartfelt thanks for the kindness shown to me and the great pains taken by you in the preparation of your address. You have really put us under a heavy debt of gratitude.

Yours sincerely,<br>Har Bhagwan

*P.S.*—Kindly send the copies of the address by passenger train as soon as it is printed, so that copies may be sent to the Press for publication.

Accordingly I handed over my manuscript to the printer with an order to print 1,000 copies. Eight days later, I received another letter from Mr. Har Bhagwan which I reproduce below :

Lahore, 22-4-36

Dear Dr. Ambedkar,

We are in receipt of your telegram and letter, for which kindly accept our thanks. In accordance with your desire, we have again postponed our Conference, but feel that it would have been much better to have it on the 25th and 26th, as the weather is growing warmer and warmer every day in the Punjab. In the middle of May it would be fairly hot, and the sittings in the day time would not be very pleasant and comfortable. However, we shall try our best to do all we can to make things as comfortable as possible, if it is held in the middle of May.

There is, however, one thing that we have been compelled to bring to your kind attention. You will remember that when I pointed out to you the misgivings entertained by some of our people regarding your declaration on the subject of change of religion, you told me that it was undoubtedly outside the scope of the Mandal and that you had no intention to say anything from our platform in that connection. At the same time when the manuscript of your address was handed to me you assured me that that was the main portion of your address and that there were only two or three concluding paragraphs that you wanted to add. On receipt of the second instalment of your address we have been taken by surprise, as that would make it so lengthy, that we are afraid, very few people would read the whole of it. Besides that you have more than once stated in your address that you had decided to walk out of the fold of the Hindus and that that was your last address as a Hindu. You have also unnecessarily attacked the morality and reasonableness of the *Vedas* and other religious books of the Hindus, and have at length dwelt upon the technical side of Hindu religion, which has absolutely no connection with the problem at issue, so much so that some of the passages have become irrelevant and off the point. We would have been very pleased if you had confined your address to that portion given to me, or if an addition was necessary, it would have been limited to what you had written on Brahminism etc. The last portion which deals with the complete annihilation of Hindu religion and doubts the morality of the sacred books of the Hindus as well as a hint about your intention to leave the Hindu fold does not seem to me to be relevant.

I would therefore most humbly request you on behalf of the people responsible for the Conference to leave out the passages referred to above, and close the address with what was given to me or add a few paragraphs on Brahminism. We doubt the wisdom of making the address unnecessarily provocative and pinching. There are several of us who subscribe to your feelings and would very much want to be under your banner for remodelling of the Hindu religion. If you had decided to get together persons of your cult I can assure you a large number would have joined your army of reformers from the Punjab.

In fact, we thought you would give us a lead in the destruction of the evil of caste system, especially when you have studied the subject so thoroughly, and strengthen our hands by bringing about a revolution and making yourself as a nucleus in the gigantic effort, but declaration of the nature made by you when repeated loses its power, and becomes a hackneyed term. Under the circumstances, I would request you to consider the whole matter and make your address more effective by saying that you would be glad to take a leading part in the destruction of the caste system if the Hindus are willing to work in right earnest toward that end, even if they had to forsake their kith and kin and the religious notions. In case you do so, I am sanguine that you would find a ready response from the Punjab in such an endeavour.

I shall be grateful if you will help us at this juncture as we have already undergone much expenditure and have been put to suspence, and let us know by the return of post that you have condescended to limit your address as above. In case, you still insist upon the printing of the address *in toto,* we very much regret it would not be possible—rather advisable for us to hold the Conference, and would prefer to postpone it *sine die,* although by doing so we shall be losing the goodwill of the people because of the repeated postponements. We should, however, like to point out that you have carved a niche in our hearts by writing such a wonderful treatise on the caste system, which excels all other treatises so far written and will prove to be a valuable heritage, so to say. We shall be ever indebted to you for the pains taken by you in its preparation.

Thanking you very much for your kindness and with best wishes.

I am, yours sincerely,
Har Bhagwan

To this letter I sent the following reply :

27th April 1936

Dear Mr. Har Bhagwan,

I am in receipt of your letter of the 22nd April. I note with regret that the Reception Committee of the Jat-Pat-Todak Mandal "would prefer to postpone the Conference *sine die*" if I insisted upon printing the address *in toto*. In reply I have to inform you that I also would prefer to have the Conference cancelled—I do not like to use vague terms—if the Mandal insisted upon having my address pruned to suit its circumstances. You may not like my decision. But I cannot give up, for the sake of the honour of presiding over the Conference, the liberty which every President must have in the preparation of the address. I cannot give up for the sake of pleasing the Mandal the duty which every President owes to the Conference over which he presides to give it a lead which he thinks right and proper. The issue is one of principle and I feel I must do nothing to compromise it in any way.

I would not have entered into any controversy as regards the propriety of the decision taken by the Reception Committee. But as you have given certain reasons which appear to throw the blame on me. I am bound to answer them. In the first place, I must dispel the notion that the views contained in that part of the address to which objection has been taken by the Committee have come to the Mandal as a surprise. Mr. Sant Ram, I am sure, will bear me out when I say that in reply to one of his letters I had said that the real method of breaking up the Caste System was not to bring about inter-caste dinners and inter-caste marriages but to destroy the religious notions on which Caste was founded and that Mr. Sant Ram in return asked me to explain what he said was a novel point of view. It was in response to this invitation from Mr. Sant Ram that I thought I ought to elaborate in my address what I had stated in a sentence in my letter to him. You cannot, therefore, say that the views expressed are new. At any rate, they are not new to Mr. Sant Ram who is the moving spirit and the leading light of your Mandal. But I go further and say that I wrote this part of my address not merely because I felt it desirable to do so. I wrote it because I thought that it was absolutely necessary to complete the argument. I am amazed to read that you characterize the portion of the speech to which your Committee objects as "irrelevant and off the point". You will allow me to say that I am a lawyer and I know the rules of relevancy as well as any member of your Committee. I most emphatically maintain that the portion objected to is not only most relevant but is also important. It is in that part of the address that I have discussed the ways and means of breaking up the Caste System. It may be that the conclusion I have arrived at as to the best method of destroying Caste is startling and painful. You are entitled to say that my analysis is wrong. But you cannot say that in an address which deals with the problem of Caste it is not open to me to discuss how Caste can be destroyed.

Your other complaint relates to the length of the address. I have pleaded guilty to the charge in the address itself. But, who is really responsible for this ? I fear you have come rather late on the scene. Otherwise you would have known that originally I had planned to write a short address for my own convenience as I had neither the time nor the energy to engage myself in the preparation of an elaborate thesis. It was the Mandal who asked me to deal with the subject exhaustively and it was the Mandal which sent down to me a list of questions relating to the Caste System and asked me to answer them in the body of my address as they were questions which were often raised in the controversy between the Mandal and its opponents and which the Mandal found difficult to answer satisfactorily. It was in trying to meet the wishes of the Mandal in this respect that the address has grown to the length to which it has. In view of what I have said I am sure you will agree that the fault respecting length of the address is not mine.

I did not expect that your Mandal would be so upset because I have spoken of the destruction of Hindu Religion. I thought it was only fools who were afraid of words. But lest there should be any misapprehension in the minds of the people I have taken great pains to explain what I mean by religion and destruction of religion. I am sure that nobody on reading my address could possibly misunderstand me. That your Mandal should have taken a fright at mere words as "destruction of religion etc." notwithstanding the explanation that accompanies, them does not raise the Mandal in my estimation. One cannot have any respect or regard for men who take the position of the Reformer and then refuse even to see the logical consequences of that position, let alone following them out in action.

You will agree that I have never accepted to be limited in any way in the preparation of my address and the question as to what the address should or should not contain was never even discussed between myself and the Mandal. I had always taken for granted that I was free to express in the address such views as I held on the subject. Indeed until, you came to Bombay on the 9th April the Mandal did not know what sort of an address I was preparing. It was when you came to Bombay that I voluntarily told you that I had no desire to use your platform from which to advocate my views regarding change of religion by the Depressed Classes. I think I have scrupulously kept that promise in the preparation of the address. Beyond a passing reference of an indirect character where I say that "I am sorry I will not be here. . . etc." I have said nothing about the subject in my address. When I see you object even to such a passing and so indirect a reference, I feel bound to ask ; did you think that in agreeing to preside over your Conference I would be agreeing to suspend or to give up my views regarding change of faith by the Depressed Classes ? If you did think so I must tell you that I am in no way responsible for such a mistake on your part. If any of you had even hinted to me that in exchange for the honour you were doing me by electing as President, I was to abjure my faith in my programme of conversion, I would have told you in quite plain terms that I cared more for my faith than for any honour from you.

After your letter of the 14th, this letter of yours comes as a surprize to me. I am sure that any one who reads them will feel the same. I cannot account for this sudden *volte face* on the part of the Reception Committee. There is no difference in substance between the rough draft which was before the Committee when you wrote your letter of the 14th and the final draft on which the decision of the Committee communicated to me in your letter under reply was taken. You cannot point out a single new idea in the final draft which is not contained in the earlier draft. The ideas are the same. The only difference is that they have been worked out in greater detail in the final draft. If there was anything to object to in the address you could have said so on the 14th. But you did not. On the contrary you asked me to print off 1,000 copies leaving me the liberty to accept or not the verbal changes which you suggested. Accordingly I got 1,000 copies printed which are now lying with me. Eight days later you write to say that you object to the address and that if it is not amended the Conference will be cancelled. You ought to have known that there was no hope of any alteration being made in the address. I told you when you were in Bombay that I would not alter a comma, that I would not allow any censorship over my address and that you would have to accept the address as it came from me. I also told you that the responsibility for the views expressed in the address was entirely mine and if they were not liked by the Conference I would not mind at all if the Conference passed a resolution condemning them. So anxious was I to relieve your Mandal from having to assume responsibility for my views and also with the object of not getting myself entangled by too intimate an association with your Conference, I suggested to you that I desired to have my address treated as a sort of an inaugural address and not as a Presidential address and that the Mandal should find some one else to preside over the Conference, and deal with the resolutions. Nobody could have been better placed to take a decision on the 14th than your Committee. The Committee failed to do that and in the meantime cost of printing has been incurred which, I am sure, with a little more firmness on the part of your Committee could have been saved.

I feel sure that the views expressed in my address have little to do with the decision of your Committee. I have reasons to believe that my presence at the Sikh Prachar Conference held at Amritsar has had a good deal to do with the decision of the Committee. Nothing else can satisfactorily explain the sudden *volte face* shown by the Committee between the 14th and the 22nd April. I must not however prolong this controversy and must request you to announce immediately that the Session of the Conference which was to meet under my Presidentship is cancelled. All the grace has by now run out and I shall not consent to preside even if your Committee agreed to accept my address as it is *in toto*. I thank you for your appreciation of the pains I have taken in the preparation of the address. I certainly have profited by the labour if no one else does. My only regret is that I was put to such hard labour at a time when my health was not equal to the strain it has caused.

Yours sincerely,<br>B. R. AMBEDKAR

This correspondence will disclose the reasons which have led to the cancellation by the Mandal of my appointment as President and the reader will be in a position to lay the blame where it ought properly to belong. This is I believe the first time when the appointment of a President is cancelled by the Reception Committee because it does not approve of the views of the President. But whether that is so or not, this is certainly the first time in my life to have been invited to preside over a Conference of Caste Hindus. I am sorry that it has ended in a tragedy. But what can any one expect from a relationship so tragic as the relationship between the reforming sect of Caste Hindus and the self-respecting sect of Untouchables where the former have no desire to alienate their orthodox fellows and the latter have no alternative but to insist upon reform being carried out?

Rajgriha, Dadar, Bombay 14
15th May 1936 **B. R. AMBEDKAR**

# SPEECH PREPARED

BY

## Dr. B.R. AMBEDKAR

FOR

### The 1936 Annual Conference of the Jat-Pat-Todak Mandal of Lahore

BUT

## NOT DELIVERED

*Owing to the cancellation of the Conference by the Reception Committee on the ground that the views expressed in the Speech would be unbearable to the Conference*

Friends,

I am really sorry for the members of the Jat-Pat-Todak Mandal who have so very kindly invited me to preside over this Conference. I am sure they will be asked many questions for having selected me as the President. The Mandal will be asked to explain as to why it has imported a man from Bombay to preside over a function which is held in Lahore. I believe the Mandal could easily have found some one better qualified than myself to preside on the occasion. I have criticised the Hindus. I have questioned the authority of the Mahatma whom they revere. They hate me. To them I am a snake in their garden. The Mandal will no doubt be asked by the politically-minded Hindus to explain why it has called me to fill this place of honour. It is an act of great daring. I shall not be surprised if some political Hindus regard it as an insult. This selection of mine cannot certainly please the ordinary religiously-minded Hindus. The Mandal may be asked to explain why it has disobeyed the *Shastric* injunction in selecting the President. Accoding to the *Shastras* the Brahmin is appointed to be the Guru for the three *Varnas,* वर्णानाम् ब्राह्मणो गुरु, is a direction of the *Shastras*. The Mandal therefore knows from whom a Hindu should take his lessons and from whom he should not. The *Shastras* do not permit a Hindu to accept any one as his Guru merely because he is well-versed. This is made very clear by Ramdas, a Brahmin saint from Maharashtra, who is alleged to have inspired Shivaji to establish a Hindu Raj. In his *Dasbodh,* a socio-politico-religious treatise in Marathi verse *Ramdas* asks, addressing the Hindus, can we accept an Antyaja to be our Guru because he is a Pandit (i.e. *learned)* and gives an answer in the negative. What replies to give to these questions is a matter which I must leave to the Mandal. The Mandal knows best the reasons which led it to travel to Bombay to select a president, to fix upon a man so repugnant to the Hindus and to descend so low in the scale as to select an Antyaja— an untouchable—to address an audience of the *Savarnas.* As for myself you will allow me to say that I have accepted the invitation much against my will and also against the will of many of my fellow untouchables. I know that the Hindus are sick of me. I know that I am not a *persona grata* with them. Knowing all this I have deliberately kept myself away from them. I have no desire to inflict myself upon them. I have been giving expression to my views from my own platform. This has already caused a great deal of heartburning and irritation. I have no desire to ascend the platform of the Hindus to do within their sight what I have been doing within their hearing. If I am here it is because of your choice and not because of my wish. Yours is a cause of social reform. That cause has always made an appeal to me and it is because of this that I felt I ought not to refuse an opportunity of helping the cause especially when you think that I can help it. Whether what I am going to say today will help you in any way to solve the problem you are grappling with is for you to judge. All I hope to do is to place before you my views on the problem.

## II

The path of social reform like the path to heaven at any rate in India, is strewn with many difficulties. Social reform in India has few friends and many critics. The critics fall into two distinct classes. One class consists of political reformers and the other of the socialists.

It was at one time recognized that without social efficiency no permanent progress in the other fields of activity was possible, that owing to mischief wrought by the evil customs, Hindu Society was not in a state of efficiency and that ceaseless efforts must be made to eradicate these evils. It was due to the recognition of this fact that the birth of the National Congress was accompanied by the foundation of the Social Conference. While the Congress was concerned with defining the weak points in the political organisation of the country, the Social Conference was engaged in removing the weak points in the social organisation of the Hindu Society. For some time the Congress and the Conference worked as two wings of one common activity and they held their annual sessions in the same pandal. But soon the two wings developed into two parties, a Political Reform Party and a Social Reform Party, between whom there raged a fierce controversy. The Political Reform Party supported the National Congress and Social Reform Party supported the Social Conference. The two bodies thus became two hostile camps. The point at issue was whether social reform should precede political reform. For a decade the forces were evenly balanced and the battle was fought without victory to either side. It was however evident that the fortunes of the Social Conference were ebbing fast. The gentlemen who presided over the sessions of the Social Conference lamented that the majority of the educated Hindus were for political advancement and indifferent to social reform and that while the number of those who attended the Congress was very large and the number who did not attend but who sympathized with it even larger, the number of those who attended the Social Conference was very much smaller. This indifference, this thinning of its ranks was soon followed by active hostility from the politicians. Under the leadership of the late Mr. Tilak, the courtesy with which the Congress allowed the Social Conference the use of its pandal was withdrawn and the spirit of enmity went to such a pitch that when the Social Conference desired to erect its own pandal a threat to burn the pandal was held out by its opponents. Thus in course of time the party in favour of political reform won and the Social Conference vanished and was forgotten. The speech, delivered by Mr. W.C. Bonnerji in 1892 at Allahabad as President of the eighth session of the Congress, sounds like a funeral oration at the death of the Social Conference and is so typical of the Congress attitude that I venture to quote from it the following extract. Mr. Bonnerji said :

> "I for one have no patience with those who say we shall not be fit for political reform until we reform our social system. I fail to see any connection between the two. . .Are we not fit (for political reform) because our widows remain unmarried and our girls are given in marriage earlier than in other countries ? because our wives and daughters do not drive about with us visiting our friends ? because we do not send our daughters to Oxford and Cambridge ?" (Cheers)

I have stated the case for political reform as put by Mr. Bonnerji. There were many who are happy that the victory went to the Congress. But those who believe in the importance of social reform may ask, is the argument such as that of Mr. Bonnerji final ? Does it prove that the victory went to those who were in the right ? Does it prove conclusively that social reform has no bearing on political reform ? It will help us to understand the matter if I state the other side of the case. I will draw upon the treatment of the untouchables for my facts.

Under the rule of the Peshwas in the Maratha country the untouchable was not allowed to use the public streets if a Hindu was coming along lest he should pollute the Hindu by his shadow. The untouchable was required to have a black thread either on his wrist or in his neck as a sign or a mark to prevent the Hindus from getting themselves polluted by his touch through mistake. In Poona, the capital of the Peshwa, the untouchable was required to carry, strung from his waist, a broom to sweep away from behind the dust he treaded on lest a Hindu walking on the same should be polluted. In Poona, the untouchable was required to carry an earthen pot, hung in his neck wherever he went, for holding his spit lest his spit falling on earth should pollute a Hindu who might unknowingly happen to tread on it. Let me take more recent facts. The tyranny practised by the Hindus upon the Balais, an untouchable community in Central India, will serve my purpose. You will find a report of this in the *Times of India* of 4th January 1928. The correspondent of the *Times of India* reported that high caste Hindus, viz. Kalotas, Rajputs and Brahmins including the Patels and Patwaris of villages of Kanaria, Bicholi-Hafsi, Bicholi-Mardana and of about 15 other villages in the Indore district (of the Indore State) informed the Balais of their respective villages that if they wished to live among them they must conform to the following rules :

(1) Balais must not wear gold-lace-bordered pugrees.

(2) They must not wear dhotis with coloured or fancy borders.

(3) They must convey intimation of the death of any Hindu to relatives of the deceased—no matter how far away these relatives may be living.

(4) In all Hindu marriages, Balais must play music before the processions and during the marriage.

(5) Balai women must not wear gold or silver ornaments; they must not wear fancy gowns or jackets.

(6) Balai women must attend all cases of confinement of Hindu women.

(7) Balais must render services without demanding remuneration and must accept whatever a Hindu is pleased to give.

(8) If the Balais do not agree to abide by these terms they must clear out of the villages. The Balais refused to comply ; and the Hindu element proceeded against them. Balais were not allowed to get water from the village wells; they were not allowed to let go their cattle to graze. Balais were prohibited from passing through land owned by a Hindu, so that if the field of a Balai was surrounded by fields owned by Hindus, the Balai could have no access to his own field. The Hindus also let their cattle graze down the fields of Balais. The Balais submitted petitions to the Darbar against these persecutions ; but as they could get no timely relief, and the oppression continued, hundreds of Balais with their wives and children were obliged to abandon their homes in which their ancestors lived for generations and to migrate to adjoining States, viz. to villages in Dhar, Dewas, Bagli, Bhopal, Gwalior and other States. What happened to them in their new homes may for the present be left out of our consideration. The incident at Kavitha in Gujarat happened only last year. The Hindus of Kavitha ordered the untouchables not to insist upon sending their children to the common village school maintained by Government. What sufferings the untouchables of Kavitha had to undergo for daring to exercise a civic right against the wishes of the Hindus is too well known to need detailed description. Another instance occurred in the village of Zanu in the Ahmedabad district of Gujarat. In November 1935 some untouchable women of well-to-do families started fetching water in metal pots. The Hindus looked upon the use of metal pots by untouchables as an affront to their dignity and assaulted the untouchable women for their impudence. A most recent event is reported from the village Chakwara in Jaipur State. It seems from the reports that have appeared in the newspapers that an untouchable of Chakwara who had returned from a pilgrimage had arranged to give a dinner to his fellow untouchables of the village as an act of religious piety. The host desired to treat the guests to a sumptuous meal and the items served included *ghee* (butter) also. But while the assembly of untouchables was engaged in partaking of the food, the Hindus in their hundreds, armed with lathis, rushed to the scene, despoiled the food and belaboured the untouchables who

left the food they were served with and ran away for their lives. And why was this murderous assault committed on defenceless untouchables ? The reason given is that the untouchable host was impudent enough to serve ghee and his untouchable guests were foolish enough to taste it. Ghee is undoubtedly a luxury for the rich. But no one would think that consumption of ghee was a mark of high social status. The Hindus of Chakwara thought otherwise and in righteous indignation avenged themselves for the wrong done to them by the untouchables, who insulted them by treating ghee as an item of their food which they ought to have known could not be theirs, consistently with the dignity of the Hindus. This means that an untouchable must not use ghee even if he can afford to buy it, since it is an act of arrogance towards the Hindus. This happened on or about the 1st of April 1936 !

Having stated the facts, let me now state the case for social reform. In doing this, I will follow Mr. Bonnerji, as nearly as I can and ask the political-minded Hindus "Are you fit for political power even though you do not allow a large class of your own countrymen like the untouchables to use public school ? Are you fit for political power even though you do not allow them the use of public wells ? Are you fit for political power even though you do not allow them the use of public streets ? Are you fit for political power even though you do not allow them to wear what apparel or ornaments they like ? Are you fit for political power even though you do not allow them to eat any food they like ?" I can ask a string of such questions. But these will suffice. I wonder what would have been the reply of Mr. Bonnerji. I am sure no sensible man will have the courage to give an affirmative answer. Every Congressman who repeats the dogma of Mill that one country is not fit to rule another country must admit that one class is not fit to rule another class.

How is it then that the Social Reform Party lost the battle ? To understand this correctly it is necessary, to take note of the kind of social reform which the reformers were agitating for. In this connection it is necessary to make a distinction between social reform in the sense of the reform of the Hindu Family and social reform in the sense of the reorganization and reconstruction of the Hindu Society. The former has relation to widow remarriage, child marriage etc., while the latter relates to the abolition of the Caste System. The Social Conference was a body which mainly concerned itself with the reform of the high caste Hindu Family. It consisted mostly of enlightened high caste Hindus who did not feel the necessity for agitating for the abolition of caste or had not the courage to agitate for it. They felt quite naturally a greater urge to remove such evils as enforced widowhood, child marriages etc., evils which prevailed among them and which were personally felt by them. They did not stand up for the reform of the *Hindu* society. The battle that was fought centered round the question of the reform of the family. It did not relate to the social reform in the sense of the break-up of the caste system. It was never put in issue by the reformers. That is the reason why the Social Reform Party lost.

I am aware that this argument cannot alter the fact that political reform did in fact gain precedence over social reform. But the argument has this much value if not more. It explains why social reformers lost the battle. It also helps us to understand how limited was the victory which the Political Reform Party obtained over the Social Reform Party and that the view that social reform need not precede political reform is a view which may stand only when by social reform is meant the reform of the family. That political reform cannot with impunity take precedence over social reform in the sense of reconstruction of society is a thesis which, I am sure, cannot be controverted. That the makers of political constitutions must take account of social forces is a fact which is recognized by no less a person than Ferdinand Lassalle, the friend and co-worker of Karl Marx. In addressing a Prussian audience in 1862 Lassalle said :

> *"The constitutional questions are in the first instance not questions of right but questions of might. The actual constitution of a country has its existence only in the actual condition of force which exists in the country : hence political constitutions have value and permanence only when they accurately express those conditions of forces which exist in practice within a society."*

But it is not necessary to go to Prussia. There is evidence at home. What is the significance of the Communal Award with its allocation of political power in defined proportions to diverse classes and communities ? In my view, its significance lies in this that political constitution must take note of social organisation. It shows that the politicians who denied that the social problem in India had any bearing on the political problem were forced to reckon with the social problem in devising the constitution. The Communal Award is so to say the nemesis following upon the indifference and neglect of social reform. It is a victory for the Social Reform Party which shows that though defeated they were in the right in insisting upon the importance of social reform. Many, I know, will not accept this finding. The view is current, and it is pleasant to believe in it, that the Communal Award is unnatural and that it is the result of an unholy alliance between the minorities and the bureaucracy. I do not wish to rely on the Communal Award as a piece of evidence to support my contention if it is said that it is not good evidence. Let us turn to Ireland. What does the history of Irish Home Rule show ? It is well-known that in the course of the negotiations between the representatives of Ulster and Southern Ireland, Mr. Redmond, the representative   Ireland, in order to bring Ulster in a Home Rule Constitution common to the whole of Ireland said to the representatives of Ulster: "Ask any political safeguards you like and you shall have them" What was the reply that Ulstermen gave? Their reply was "Damn your safeguards, we don't want to be ruled by you on any terms." People who blame the minorities in India ought to consider what would have happened to the political aspirations of the majority if the minorities had taken the attitude which. Ulster took. Judged by the attitude of Ulster to Irish Home Rule, is it nothing that the minorities agreed to be ruled by the majority which has not shown much sense of statesmanship, provided some safeguards were devised for them? But this is only incidental. The main question is why did Ulster take this attitude? The only answer I can give is that there was a social problem between Ulster and Southern Ireland the problem between Catholics and Protestants, essentially a problem of Caste. That Home Rule in Ireland would be Rome Rule was the way in which the Ulstermen had framed their answer. But that is only another way of stating that it was the social problem of Caste between the Catholics and Protestants, which prevented the solution of the political problem. This evidence again is sure to be challenged. It will be urged that here too the hand of the Imperialist was at work. But my resources are not exhausted. I will give evidence from the History of Rome. Here no one can say that any evil genius was at work. Any one who has studied the History of Rome will know that the Republican Constitution of Rome bore marks having strong resemblance to the Communal Award. When the kingship in Rome was abolished, the Kingly power or the *Imperium* was divided between the Consuls and the Pontifex Maximus. In the Consuls was vested the secular authority of the King, while the latter took over the religious authority of King. This Republican Constitution had provided that, of the two Consuls one was to be Patrician and the other Plebian. The same constitution had also provided that, of the Priests under the Pontifex Maximus, half were to be Plebians and the other half Patricians. Why is it that the Republican Constitution of Rome had these provisions which, as I said, resemble so strongly the provisions of the Communal Award? The only answer one can get is that the Constitution of Republican Rome had to take account of the social division between the Patricians and the Plebians, who formed two distinct castes. To sum up, let political reformers turn to any direction they like, they will find that in the making of a constitution, they cannot ignore the problem arising out of the prevailing social order.

The illustrations which I have taken in support of the proposition that social and religious problems have a bearing on political constitutions seem to be too particular. Perhaps they are. But it should not be supposed that the bearing of the one on the other is limited. On the other hand one can say that generally speaking History bears out the proposition that political revolutions have always been preceded by social and religious revolutions.

The religious Reformation started by Luther was the precursor of the political emancipation of the European people. In England Puritanism led to the establishment of political liberty. Puritanism founded the new world. It was Puritanism which won the war of American Independence and Puritanism was a religious movement. The same is true of the Muslim Empire. Before the Arabs became a political power they had undergone a thorough religious revolution started by the Prophet Mohammad. Even Indian History supports the same conclusion. The political revolution led by Chandragupta was preceded by the religious and social revolution of Buddha. The political revolution led by Shivaji was preceded by the religious and social reform brought about by the saints of Maharashtra. The political revolution of the Sikhs was preceded by the religious and social revolution led by Guru Nanak. It is unnecessary to add more illustrations. These will suffice to show that the emancipation of the mind and the soul is a necessary preliminary for the political expansion of the people.

### III

Let me now turn to the Socialists. Can the Socialists ignore the problem arising out of the social order ? The Socialists of India following their fellows in Europe are seeking to apply the economic interpretation of history to the facts of India. They propound that man is an economic creature, that his activities and aspirations are bound by economic facts, that property is the only source of power. They, therefore, preach that political and social reforms are but gigantic illusions and that economic reform by equalization of property must have precedence over every other kind of reform. One may join issue on every one of these premises on which rests the Socialists' case for economic reform having priority over every other kind of reform. One may contend that economic motive is not the only motive by which man is actuated. That economic power is the only kind of power no student of human society can accept. That the social status of an individual by itself often becomes a source of power and authority is made clear by the sway which the Mahatmas have held over the common man. Why do millionaires in India obey penniless Sadhus and Fakirs ? Why do millions of paupers in India sell their trifling trinckets which constitute their only wealth and go to Benares and Mecca ? That, religion is the source of power is illustrated by the history of India where the priest holds a sway over the common man often greater than the magistrate and where everything, even such things as strikes and elections, so easily take a religious turn and can so easily be given a religious twist. Take the case of the Plebians of Rome as a further illustration of the power of religion over man. It throws great light on this point. The Plebs had fought for a share in the supreme executive under the Roman Republic and had secured the appointment of a Plebian Consul elected by a separate electorate constituted by the *Commitia Centuriata,* which was an assembly of Plebians. They wanted a Consul of their own because they felt that the Patrician Consuls used to discriminate against the Plebians in carrying on the administration. They had apparently obtained a great gain because under the Republican Constitution of Rome one Consul had the power of vetoing an act of the other Consul. But did they in fact gain anything? The answer to this question must be in the negative. The Plebians never could get a Plebian Consul who could be said to be a strong man and who could act independently of the Patrician Consul. In the ordinary course of things the Plebians should have got a strong Plebian Consul in view of the fact that his election was to be by a separate electorate of Plebians. The question is why did they fail in getting a strong Plebian to officiate as their Consul? The answer to this question reveals the dominion which religion exercises over the minds of men. It was an accepted creed of the whole Roman *populus* that no official could enter upon the duties of his office unless the Oracle of Delphi declared that he was acceptable to the Goddess. The priests who were in charge of the temple of the Goddess of Delphi were all Patricians. Whenever therefore the Plebians elected a Consul who was known to be a strong party man opposed to the Patricians or "communal" to use the term that is current in India, the Oracle invariably declared that he was not acceptable to the Goddess. This is how the Plebians were cheated out of their rights. But what is worthy of note is that the Plebians permitted themselves to be thus cheated because they too like the Patricians, held firmly the belief that the approval of the Goddess was a condition precedent to the taking charge by an official of his duties and that election by the people was not enough. If the Plebians had contended that election was enough and that the approval by the Goddess was not necessary they would have derived the fullest benefit from the political right which they had obtained. But they did not. They agreed to elect another, less suitable to themselves but more suitable to the Goddess which in fact meant more amenable to the Patricians. Rather than give up religion, the Plebians give up material gain for which they had fought so hard. Does this not show that religion can be a source of power as great as money if not greater? The fallacy of the Socialists lies in supposing that because in the present stage of European Society property as a source of power is predominant, that the same is true of India or that the same was true of Europe in the past. Religion, social status and property are all sources of power and authority, which one man has, to control the liberty of another. One is predominant at one stage, the other is predominant at another stage. That is the only difference. If liberty is the ideal, if liberty means the destruction of the dominion which one man holds over another then obviously it cannot be insisted upon that economic reform must be the one kind of reform worthy of pursuit. If the source of power and dominion is at any given time or in any given society social and religious then social reform and religious reform must be accepted as the necessary sort of reform.

One can thus attack the doctrine of Economic Interpretation of History adopted by the Socialists of India. But I recognize that economic interpretation of history is not necessary for the validity of the Socialist contention that equalization of property is the only real reform and that it must precede everything else. However, what I like to ask the Socialists is this : Can you have economic reform without first bringing about a reform of the social order ? The Socialists of India do not seem to have considered this question. I do not wish to do them an injustice. I give below a quotation from a letter which a prominent Socialist wrote a few days ago to a friend of mine in which he said, "I do not believe that we can build up a free society in India so long as there is a trace of this ill-treatment and suppression of one class by another. Believing as I do in a socialist ideal, inevitably I believe in perfect equality in the treatment of various classes and groups. I think that Socialism offers the only true remedy for this as well as other problems." Now the question that I like to ask is : Is it enough for a Socialist to say, "I believe in perfect equality in the treatment of the various classes ?" To say that such a belief is enough is to disclose a complete lack of understanding of what is involved in Socialism. If Socialism is a practical programme and is not merely an ideal, distant and far off, the question for a Socialist is not whether he believes in equality. The question for him is whether he *minds* one class ill-treating and suppressing another class as a matter of system, as a matter of principle and thus allow tyranny and oppression to continue to divide one class from another. Let me analyse the factors that are involved in the realization of Socialism in order to explain fully my point. Now it is obvious that the economic reform contemplated by the Socialists cannot come about unless there is a revolution resulting in the seizure of power. That seizure of power must be by a proletariat. The first question I ask is : Will the proletariat of India combine to bring about this revolution ? What will move men to such an action ? It seems to me that other things being equal the only thing that will move one man to take such an action is the feeling that other man with whom he is acting are actuated by feeling of equality and fraternity and above all of justice. Men will not join in a revolution for the equalization of property unless they know that after the revolution is achieved they will be treated equally and that there will be no discrimination of caste and creed. The assurance of a socialist leading the revolution that he does not believe in caste, I am sure, will not suffice. The assurance must be the assurance proceeding from much deeper foundation, namely, the mental attitude of the compatriots towards one another in their spirit of personal equality and fraternity. Can it be said that the proletariat of India, poor as it is, recognise no distinctions except that of the rich and the poor ? Can it be said that the poor in India recognize no such distinctions of caste or creed, high or low ? If the fact is that they do, what unity of front can be expected from such a proletariat in its action against the rich ? How can there be a revolution if the proletariat cannot present a united front? Suppose for the sake of argument that by some freak of fortune a revolution does take place and the Socialists come in power, will they not have to deal with the problems created by the particular social order prevalent in India ? I can't see how a Socialist State in India can function for a second without having to grapple with the problems created by the prejudices which make Indian people observe the distinctions of high and low, clean and unclean. If Socialists are not to be content with the mouthing of fine phrases, if the Socialists wish to make Socialism a definite reality then they must recognize that the problem of social reform is fundamental and that for them there is no escape from it. That, the social order prevalent in India is a matter which a Socialist must deal with, that unless he does so he cannot achieve his revolution and that if he does achieve it as a result of good fortune he will have to grapple with it if he wishes to realize his ideal, is a proposition which in my opinion is incontrovertible. He will be compelled to take account of caste after revolution if he does not take account of it before revolution. This is only another way of saying that, turn in any direction you like, caste is the monster that crosses your path. You cannot have political reform, you cannot have economic reform, unless you kill this monster.

## IV

It is a pity that Caste even today has its defenders. The defences are many. It is defended on the ground that the Caste System is but another name for division of labour and if division of labour is a necessary feature of every civilized society then it is argued that there is nothing wrong in the Caste System. Now the first thing is to be urged against this view is that Caste System is not merely division of labour. *It is also a division of labourers.* Civilized society undoubtedly needs division of labour. But in no civilized society is division of labour accompanied by this unnatural division of labourers into water-tight compartments. Caste System is not merely a division of labourers which is quite different from division of labour—it is an heirarchy in which the divisions of labourers are graded one above the other. In no other country is the division of labour accompanied by this gradation of labourers. There is also a third point of criticism against this view of the Caste System. This division of labour is not spontaneous, it is not based on natural aptitudes. Social and individual efficiency requires us to develop the capacity of an individual to the point of competency to choose and to make his own career. This principle is violated in the Caste System in so far as it involves an attempt to appoint tasks to individuals in advance, selected not on the basis of trained original capacities, but on that of the social status of the parents. Looked at from another point of view this stratification of occupations which is the result of the Caste System is positively pernicious. Industry is never static. It undergoes rapid and abrupt changes. With such changes an individual must be free to change his occupation. Without such freedom to adjust himself to changing circumstances it would be impossible for him to gain his livelihood. Now the Caste System will not allow Hindus to take to occupations where they are wanted if they do not belong to them by heredity. If a Hindu is seen to starve rather than take to new occupations not assigned to his Caste, the reason is to be found in the Caste System. By not permitting readjustment of occupations, caste becomes a direct cause of much of the unemployment we see in the country. As a form of division of labour the Caste system suffers from another serious defect. The division of labour brought about by the Caste System is not a division based on choice. Individual sentiment, individual preference has no place in it. It is based on the dogma of predestination. Considerations of social efficiency would compel us to recognize that the greatest evil in the industrial system is not so much poverty and the suffering that it involves as the fact that so many persons have callings which make no appeal to those who are engaged in them. Such callings constantly provoke one to aversion, ill-will and the desire to evade. There are many occupations in India which on account of the fact that they are regarded as degraded by the Hindus provoke those who are engaged in them to aversion. There is a constant desire to evade and escape from such occupations which arises solely because of the blighting effect which they produce upon those who follow them owing to the slight and stigma cast upon them by the Hindu religion. What efficiency can there be in a system under which neither men's hearts nor their minds are in their work? As an economic organization Caste is therefore a harmful institution, inasmuch as, it involves the subordination of man's natural powers and inclinations to the exigencies of social rules

## V

Some have dug a biological trench in defence of the Caste System. It is said that the object of Caste was to preserve purity of race and purity of blood. Now ethnologists are of opinion that men of pure race exist nowhere and that there has been a mixture of all races in all parts of the world. Especially is this the case with the people of India. Mr. D. R. Bhandarkar in his paper on *Foreign Elements in the Hindu Population* has stated that "There is hardly a class, or Caste in India which has not a foreign strain in it. There is an admixture of alien blood not only among the warrior classes—the Rajputs and the Marathas—but also among the Brahmins who are under the happy delusion that they are free from all foreign elements." The Caste system cannot be said to have grown as a means of preventing the admixture of races or as a means of maintaining purity of blood. As a matter of fact Caste system came into being long after the different races of India had commingled in blood and culture. To hold that distinctions of Castes or really distinctions of race and to treat different Castes as though they were so many different races is a gross perversion of facts. What racial affinity is there between the Brahmin of the Punjab and the Brahmin of Madras? What racial affinity is there between the untouchable of Bengal and the untouchable of Madras? What racial difference is there between the Brahmin of the Punjab and the Chamar of the Punjab? What racial difference is there between the Brahmin of Madras and the Pariah of Madras? The Brahmin of the Punjab is racially of the same stock as the Chamar of the Punjab and the Brahmin of Madras is of the same race as the Pariah of Madras. Caste system does not demarcate racial division. Caste system is a social division of people of the same race. Assuming it, however, to be a case of racial divisions one may ask: What harm could there be if a mixture of races and of blood was permitted to take place in India by intermarriages between different Castes? Men are no doubt divided from animals by so deep a distinction that science recognizes men and animals as two distinct species. But even scientists who believe in purity of races do not assert that the different races constitute different species of men. They are only varieties of one and the same species. As such they can interbreed and produce an offspring which is capable of breeding and which is not sterile. An immense lot of nonsense is talked about heredity and eugenics in defence of the Caste System. Few would object to the Caste System if it was in accord with the basic principle of eugenics because few can object to the improvement of the race by judicious mating. But one fails to understand how the Caste System secures judicious mating. Caste System is a negative thing. It merely prohibits persons belonging to different Castes from intermarrying. It is not a positive method of selecting which two among a given Caste should marry. If Caste is eugenic in origin then the origin of sub-Castes must also be eugenic. But can any one seriously maintain that the origin of sub-Castes is eugenic? I think it would be absurd to contend for such a proposition and for a very obvious reason. If Caste means race then differences of sub-Castes cannot mean differences of race because sub-Castes become *ex hypothesia* sub-divisions of one and the same race. Consequently the bar against intermarrying and interdining between sub-Castes cannot be for the purpose of maintaining purity of race or of blood. If sub-Castes cannot be eugenic in origin there cannot be any substance in the contention that Caste is eugenic in origin. Again if Caste is eugenic in origin one can understand the bar against intermarriage. But what is the purpose of the interdict placed on interdining between Castes and sub-Castes alike? Interdining cannot infect blood and therefore cannot be the cause either of the improvement or of deterioration of the race. This shows that Caste has no scientific origin and that those who are attempting to give it an eugenic basis are trying to support by science what is grossly unscientific. Even today eugenics cannot become a practical possibility unless we have definite knowledge regarding the laws of heredity. Prof. Batcson in his *Mendel's Principles of Heredity* says, "There is nothing in the descent of the higher mental qualities to suggest that they follow any single system of transmission. It is likely that both they and the more marked developments of physical powers result rather from the coincidence of numerous factors than from the possession of any one genetic element." To argue that the Caste System was eugenic in its conception is to attribute to the forefathers of present-day Hindus a knowledge of heredity which even the modern scientists do not possess. A tree should be judged by the fruits it yields. If caste is eugenic what sort of a race of men it should have produced? Physically speaking the Hindus are a $C_3$ people. They are a race of Pygmies and dwarfs stunted in stature and wanting in stamina. It is a nation 9/10ths of which is declared to be unfit for military service. This shows that the Caste System does not embody the eugenics of modern scientists. It is a social system which embodies the arrogance and selfishness of a perverse section of the Hindus who were superior enough in social status to set it in fashion and who had authority to force it on their inferiors.

## VI

Caste does not result in economic efficiency. Caste cannot and has not improved the race. Caste has however done one thing. It has completely disorganized and demoralized the Hindus.

The first and foremost thing that must be recognized is that Hindu Society is a myth. The name Hindu is itself a foreign name. It was given by the Mohammedans to the natives for the purpose of distinguishing themselves. It does not occur in any Sanskrit work prior to the Mohammedan invasion. They did not feel the necessity of a common name because they had no conception of their having constituted a community. Hindu society as such does not exist. It is only a collection of castes. Each caste is conscious of its existence. Its survival is the be all and end all of its existence. Castes do not even form a federation. A caste has no feeling that it is affiliated to other castes except when there is a Hindu-Muslim riot. On all other occasions each caste endeavours to segregate itself and to distinguish itself from other castes. Each caste not only dines among itself and marries among itself but each caste prescribes its own distinctive dress. What other explanation can there be of the innumerable styles of dress worn by the men and women of India which so amuse the tourists? Indeed the ideal Hindu must be like a rat living in his own hole refusing to have any contact with others. There is an utter lack among the Hindus of what the sociologists call "consciousness of kind". There is no Hindu consciousness of kind. In every Hindu the consciousness that exists is the consciousness of his caste. That is the reason why the Hindus cannot be said to form a society or a nation. There are however many Indians whose patriotism does not permit them to admit that Indians are not a nation, that they are only an amorphous mass of people. They have insisted that underlying the apparent diversity there is a fundamental unity which marks the life of the Hindus in as much as there is a similarity of habits and customs, beliefs and thoughts which obtain all over the continent of India. Similarity in habits and customs, beliefs and thoughts there is. But one cannot accept the conclusion that therefore, the Hindus constitute a society. To do so is to misunderstand the essentials which go to make up a society. Men do not become a society by living in physical proximity any more than a man ceases to be a member of his society by living so many miles away from other men. Secondly similarity in habits and customs, beliefs and thoughts is not enough to constitute men into society. Things may be passed physically from one to another like bricks. In the same way habits and customs, beliefs and thoughts of one group may be taken over by another group and there may thus appear a similarity between the two. Culture spreads by diffusion and that is why one finds similarity between various primitive tribes in the matter of their habits and customs, beliefs and thoughts, although they do not live in proximity. But no one could say that because there was this similarity the primitive tribes constituted one society. This is because similarly in certain things is not enough to constitute a society. Men constitute a society because they have things which they possess in common. To have similar thing is totally different from possessing things in common. And the only way by which men can come to possess things in common with one another is by being in communication with one another. This is merely another way of saying that Society continues to exist by communication indeed in communication. To make it concrete, it is not enough if men act in a way which agrees with the acts of others. Parallel activity, even if similar, is not sufficient to bind men into a society. This is proved by the fact that the festivals observed by the different Castes amongst the Hindus are the same. Yet these parallel performances of similar festivals by the different castes have not bound them into one integral whole. For that purpose what is necessary is for a man to share and participate in a common activity so that the same emotions are aroused in him that animate the others. Making the individual a sharer or partner in the associated activity so that he feels its success as his success, its failure as his failure is the real thing that binds men and makes a society of them. The Caste System prevents common activity and by preventing common activity it has prevented the Hindus from becoming a society with a unified life and a consciousness of its own being.

## VII

The Hindus often complain of the isolation and exclusiveness of a gang or a clique and blame them for anti-social spirit. But they conveniently forget that this anti-social spirit is the worst feature of their own Caste System. One caste enjoys singing a hymn of hate against another caste as much as the Germans did in singing their hymn of hate against the English during the last war. The literature of the Hindus is full of caste genealogies in which an attempt is made to give a noble origin to one caste and an ignoble origin to other castes. The *Sahyadrikhand* is a notorious instance of this class of literature. This anti-social spirit is not confined to caste alone. It has gone deeper and has poisoned the mutual relations of the sub-castes as well. In my province the Golak Brahmins, Deorukha Brahmins, Karada Brahmins, Palshe Brahmins and Chitpavan Brahmins, all claim to be sub-divisions of the Brahmin Caste. But the anti-social spirit that prevails between them is quite as marked and quite as virulent as the anti-social spirit that prevails between them and other non-Brahmin castes. There is nothing strange in this. An anti-social spirit is found wherever one group has "interests of its own" which shut it out from full interaction with other groups, so that its prevailing purpose is protection of what it has got. This anti-social spirit, this spirit of protecting its own interests is as much a marked feature of the different castes in their isolation from one another as it is of nations in their isolation. The Brahmin's primary concern is to protect "his interest" against those of the non-Brahmins and the non-Brahmin's primary concern is to protect their interests against those of the Brahmins. The Hindus, therefore, are not merely an assortment of castes but they are so many warring groups each living for itself and for its selfish ideal. There is another feature of caste which is deplorable. The ancestors of the present-day English fought on one side or the other in the wars of the Roses and the Cromwellian War. But the decendents of those who fought on the one side do not bear any animosity—any grudge against the descendents of those who fought on the other side. The feud is forgotten. But the present-day non-Brahmins cannot forgive the present-day Brahmins for the insult their ancestors gave to Shivaji. The present-day Kayasthas will not forgive the present-day Brahmins for the infamy cast upon their forefathers by the forefathers of the latter. To what is this difference due ? Obviously to the Caste System. The existence of Caste and Caste Consciousness has served to keep the memory of past feuds between castes green and has prevented solidarity.

## VIII

The recent discussion about the excluded and partially included areas has served to draw attention to the position of what are called the aboriginal tribes in India. They number about 13 millions if not more. Apart from the questions whether their exclusion from the new Constitution is proper or improper, the fact still remains that these aborigines have remained in their primitive uncivilized State in a land which boasts of a civilization thousands of years old. Not only are they not civilized but some of them follow pursuits which have led to their being classified as criminals. Thirteen millions of people living in the midst of civilization are still in a savage state and are leading the life of hereditary criminals ! ! But the Hindus have never felt ashamed of it. This is a phenomenon which in my view is quite unparalleled.

What is the cause of this shameful state of affairs ? Why has no attempt been made to civilize these aborigines and to lead them to take to a more honourable way of making a living ? The Hindus will probably seek to account for this savage state of the aborigines by attributing to them congenital stupidity. They will probably not admit that the aborigines have remained savages because they had made no effort to civilize them, to give them medical aid, to reform them, to make them good citizens. But supposing a Hindu wished to do what the Christian missionary is doing for these aborigines, could he have done it ? I submit not. Civilizing the aborigines means adopting them as your own, living in their midst, and cultivating fellow-feeling, in short loving them. How is it possible for a Hindu to do this ? His whole life is one anxious effort to preserve his caste. Caste is his precious possession which he must save at any cost. He cannot consent to lose it by establishing contact with the aborigines the remnants of the hateful Anaryas of the *Vedic* days. Not that a Hindu could not be taught the sense of duty to fallen humanity, but the trouble is that no amount of sense of duty can enable him to overcome his duty to preserve his caste. Caste is, therefore, the real explanation as to why the Hindu has let the savage remain a savage in the midst of his civilization without blushing or without feeling any sense of remorse or repentance. The Hindu has not realized that these aborigines are a source of potential danger. If these savages remain savages they may not do any harm to the Hindus. But if they are reclaimed by non-Hindus and converted to their faiths they will swell the ranks of the enemies of the Hindus. If this happens the Hindu will have to thank himself and his Caste System.

## IX

Not only has the Hindu made no effort for the humanitarian cause of civilizing the savages but the higher-caste Hindus have deliberately prevented the lower castes who are within the pale of Hinduism from rising to the cultural level of the higher castes. I will give two instances, one of the Sonars and the other of the Pathare Prabhus. Both are communities quite well-known in Maharashtra. Like the rest of the communities desiring to raise their status these two communities were at one time endeavouring to adopt some of the ways and habits of the Brahmins. The Sonars were styling themselves Daivadnya Brahmins and were wearing their "dhotis" with folds on and using the word *namaskar* for salutation. Both, the folded way of wearing the "dhoti" and the *namaskar* were special to the Brahmins. The Brahmins did not like this imitation and this attempt by Sonars to pass off as Brahmins. Under the authority of the Peshwas the Brahmins successfully put down this attempt on the part of the Sonars to adopt the ways of the Brahmins. They even got the President of the Councils of the East India Company's settlement in Bombay to issue a prohibitory order against the Sonars residing in Bombay. At one time the Pathare Prabhus had widow-remarriage as a custom of their caste. This custom of widow-remarriage was later on looked upon as a mark of social inferiority by some members of the caste especially because it was contrary to the custom prevalent among the Brahmins. With the object of raising the status of their community some Pathare Prabhus sought to stop this practice of widow-remarriage that was prevalent in their caste. The community was divided into two camps, one for and the other against the innovation. The Peshwas took the side of those in favour of widow-remarriage and thus virtually prohibited the Pathare Prabhus from following the ways of the Brahmins. The Hindus criticise the Mohammedans for having spread their religion by the use of the sword. They also ridicule Christianity on the score of the inquisition. But really speaking who is better and more worthy of our respect—the Mohammedans and Christians who attempted to thrust down the throats of unwilling persons what they regarded as necessary for their salvation or the Hindu who would not spread the light, who would endeavour to keep others in darkness, who would not consent to share his intellectual and social inheritance with those who are ready and willing to make it a part of their own make-up ? I have no hesitation in saying that if the Mohammedan has been cruel the Hindu has been mean and meanness is worse than cruelty.

## X

Whether the Hindu religion was or was not a missionary religion has been a controversial issue. Some hold the view that it was never a missionary religion. Others hold that it was. That the Hindu religion was once a missionary religion must be admitted. It could not have spread over the face of India, if it was not a missionary religion. That today it is not a missionary religion is also a fact which must be accepted. The question therefore is not whether or not the Hindu religion was a missionary religion. The real question is why did the Hindu religion cease to be a missionary religion ? My answer is this. Hindu religion ceased to be a missionary religion when the Caste System grew up among the Hindus. Caste is inconsistent with conversion. Inculcation of beliefs and dogmas is not the only problem that is involved in conversion. To find a place for the convert in the social life of the community is another and a much more important problem that arises in connection with conversion. That problem is where to place the convert, in what caste ? It is a problem which must baffle every Hindu wishing to make aliens converts to his religion. Unlike the club the membership of a caste is not open to all and sundry. The law of caste confines its membership to person bom in the caste. Castes are autonomous and there is no authority anywhere to compel a caste to admit a new-comer to its social life. Hindu Society being a collection of castes and each caste being a close corporation there is no place for a convert. Thus it is the caste which has prevented the Hindus from expanding and from absorbing other religious communities. So long as caste remain, Hindu religion cannot be made a missionary religion and *Shudhi* will be both a folly and a futility.

## XI

The reasons which have made *Shudhi* impossible for Hindus are also responsible for making *Sanghatan* impossible. The idea underlying *Sanghatan* is to remove from the mind of the Hindu that timidity and cowardice which so painfully make him off from the Mohammedan and the Sikh and which have led him to adopt the low ways of treachery and cunning for protecting himself. The question naturally arises : From where does the Sikh or the Mohammedan derive his strength which makes him brave and fearless ? I am sure it is not due to relative superiority of physical strength, diet or drill. It is due to the strength arising out of the feeling that all Sikhs will come to the rescue of a Sikh when he is in danger and that all Mohammedans will rush to save a Muslim if he is attacked. The Hindu can derive no such strength. He cannot feel assured that his fellows will come to his help. Being one and fated to be alone he remains powerless, develops timidity and cowardice and in a fight surrenders or runs away. The Sikh as well as the Muslim stands fearless and gives battle because he knows that though one he will not be alone. The presence of this belief in the one helps him to hold out and the absence of it in the other makes him to give way. If you pursue this matter further and ask what is it that enables the Sikh and the Mohammedan to feel so assured and why is the Hindu filled with such despair in the matter of help and assistance you will find that the reasons for this difference lie in the difference in their associated mode of living. The associated mode of life practised by the Sikhs and the Mohammedans produces fellow-feeling. The associated mode of life of the Hindus does not. Among Sikhs and Muslims there is a social cement which makes them *Bhais*. Among Hindus there is no such cement and one Hindu does not regard another Hindu as his *Bhai*. This explains why a Sikh says and feels that one Sikh, or one Khalsa is equal to *Sava Lakh* men. This explains why one Mohammedan is equal to a crowd of Hindus. This difference is undoubtedly a difference due to caste. So long as caste remains, there will be no *Sanghatan* and so long as there is no *Sanghatan* the Hindu will remain weak and meek. The Hindus claim to be a very tolerant people. In my opinion this is a mistake. On many occasions they can be intolerant and if on some occasions they are tolerant that is because they are too weak to oppose or too indifferent to oppose. This indifference of the Hindus has become so much a part of their nature that a Hindu will quite meekly tolerate an insult as well as a wrong. You see amongst them, to use the words of Morris, *"The great reading down the little, the strong heating down the weak, cruel men fearing not, kind men daring not and wise men caring not."* With the Hindu Gods all forbearing, it is not difficult to imagine the pitiable condition of the wronged and the oppressed among the Hindus. Indifferentism is the worst kind of disease that can infect a people. Why is the Hindu so indifferent? In my opinion this indifferentism is the result of Caste System which has made *Sanghatan* and co-operation even for a good cause impossible.

## XII

The assertion by the individual of his own opinions and beliefs, his own independence and interest as over against group standards, group authority and group interests is the beginning of all reform. But whether the reform will continue depends upon what scope the group affords for such individual assertion. If the group is tolerant and fair-minded in dealing with such individuals they will continue to assert and in the end succeed in converting their fellows. On the other hand if the group is intolerant and does not bother about the means it adopts to stifle such individuals they will perish and the reform will die out. New a caste has an unquestioned right to excommunicate any man who is guilty of breaking the rules of the caste and when it is realized that excommunication involves a complete cesser of social intercourse it will be agreed that as a form of punishment there is really little to choose between excommunication and death. No wonder individual Hindus have not had the courage to assert their independence by breaking the barriers of caste. It is true that man cannot get on with his fellows. But it is also true that he cannot do without them. He would like to have the society of his fellows on his terms. If he cannot get it on his terms then he will be ready to have it on any terms even amounting to complete surrender. This is because he cannot do without society. A caste is ever ready to take advantage of the helplessness of a man and insist upon complete conformity to its code in letter and in spirit. A caste can easily organize itself into a conspiracy to make the life of a reformer a hell and if a conspiracy is a crime I do not understand why such a nefarious act as an attempt to excommunicate a person for daring to act contrary to the rules of caste should not be made an offence punishable in law. But as it is, even law gives each caste an autonomy to regulate its membership and punish dissenters with excommunication. Caste in the hands of the orthodox has been a powerful weapon for persecuting the reforms and for killing all reform.

## XIII

The effect of caste on the ethics of the Hindus is simply deplorable. Caste has killed public spirit. Caste has destroyed the sense of public charity. Caste has made public opinion impossible. A Hindu's public is his caste. His responsibility is only to his caste. His loyalty is restricted only to his caste. Virtue has become caste-ridden and morality has become caste-bound. There is no sympathy to the deserving. There is no appreciation of the meritorious. There is no charity to the needy. Suffering as such calls for no response. There is charity but it begins with the caste and ends with the caste. There is sympathy but not for men of other caste. Would a Hindu acknowledge and follow the leadership of a great and good man? The case of a Mahatma apart, the answer must be that he will follow a leader if he is a man of his caste. A Brahmin will follow a leader only if he is a Brahmin, a Kayastha if he is a Kayastha and so on. The capacity to appreciate merits in a man apart from his caste does not exist in a Hindu. There is appreciation of virtue but only when the man is a fellow caste-man. The whole morality is as bad as tribal morality. My caste-man, right or wrong; my caste-man, good or bad. It is not a case of standing by virtue and not standing by vice. It is a case of standing or not standing by the caste. Have not Hindus committed treason against their country in the interests of their caste?

## XIV

I would not be surprised if some of you have grown weary listening to this tiresome tale of the sad effects which caste has produced. There is nothing new in it. I will therefore turn to the constructive side of the problem. What is your ideal society if you do not want caste is a question that is bound to be asked of you. If you ask me, my ideal would be a society based on *Liberty, Equality* and *Fraternity*. And why not? What objection can there be to Fraternity? I cannot imagine any. An ideal society should be mobile, should be full of channels for conveying a change taking place in one part to other parts. In an ideal society there should be many interests consciously communicated and shared. There should be varied and free points of contact with other modes of association. In other words there must be social endosmosis. This is fraternity, which is only another name for democracy. Democracy is not merely a form of Government. It is primarily a mode of associated living, of conjoint communicated experience. It is essentially an attitude of respect and reverence towards fellowmen. Any objection to Liberty? Few object to liberty in the sense of a right to free movement, in the sense of a right to life and limb. There is no objection to liberty in the sense of a right to property, tools and materials as being necessary for earning a living to keep the body in due state of health. Why not allow liberty to benefit by an effective and competent use of a person's powers? The supporters of caste who would allow liberty in the sense of a right to life, limb and property, would not readily consent to liberty in this sense, inasmuch as it involves liberty to choose one's profession. But to object to this kind of liberty is to perpetuate slavery. For slavery does not merely mean a legalized form of subjection. It means a state of society in which some men are forced to accept from other the purposes which control their conduct. This condition obtains even where mere is no slavery in the legal sense. It is found where, as in the Caste System, some persons are compelled to carry on certain prescribed callings which are not of their choice. Any objection to equality? This has obviously been the most contentious part of the slogan of the French

Revolution. The objections to equality may be sound and one may have to admit that all men are not equal. But what of that? Equality may be a fiction but nonetheless one must accept it as the governing principle. A man's power is dependent upon (1) physical heredity, (2) social inheritance or endowment in the form of parental care, education, accumulation of scientific knowledge, everything which enables him to be more efficient than the savage, and finally, (3) on his own efforts. In all these three respects men are undoubtedly unequal. But the question is, shall we treat them as unequal because they are unequal? This is a question which the opponents of equality must answer. From the standpoint of the individualist it may be just to treat men unequally so far as their efforts are unequal. It may be desirable to give as much incentive as possible to the full development of every one's powers. But what would happen if men were treated unequally as they are, in the first two respects? It is obvious that those individuals also in whose favour there is birth, education, family name, business connections and inherited wealth would be selected in the race. But selection under such circumstances would not be a selection of the able. It would be the selection of the privileged. The reason therefore, which forces that in the third respect we should treat men unequally demands that in the first two respects we should treat men as equally as possible. On the other hand it can be urged that if it is good for the social body to get the most out of its members, it can get most out of them only by making them equal as far as possible at the very start of the race. That is one reason why we cannot escape equality. But there is another reason why we must accept equality. A Statesman is concerned with vast numbers of people. He has neither the time nor the knowledge to draw fine distinctions and to treat each equitably *i.e.* according to need or according to capacity. However desirable or reasonable an equitable treatment of men may be, humanity is not capable of assortment and classification. The statesman, therefore, must follow some rough and ready rule and that rough and ready rule is to treat all men alike not because they are alike but because classification and assortment is impossible. The doctrine of equality is glaringly fallacious but taking all in all it is the only way a statesman can proceed in politics which is a severely practical affair and which demands a severely practical test.

## XV

But there is a set of reformers who hold out a different ideal. They go by the name of the Arya Samajists and their ideal of social organization is what is called Chaturvarnya or the division of society into four classes instead of the four thousand castes that we have in India. To make it more attractive and to disarm opposition the protagonists of Chaturvarnya take great care to point out that their Chaturvarnya is based not on birth but on *guna* (worth). At the outset, I must confess that notwithstanding the worth-basis of this

Chaturvarnya, it is an ideal to which I cannot reconcile myself. In the first place, if under the Chaturvarnya of the Arya Samajists an individual is to take his place in the Hindu Society according to his worth. I do not understand why the Arya Samajists insist upon labelling men as Brahmin, Kshatriya, Vaishya and Shudra. A learned man would be honoured without his being labelled a Brahmin. A soldier would be respected without his being designated a Kshatriya. If European society honours its soldiers and its servants without giving them permanent labels, why should Hindu Society find it difficult to do so is a question, which Arya Samajists have not cared to consider. There is another objection to the continuance of these labels. All reform consists in a change in the notions, sentiment and mental attitudes of the people towards men and things. It is common experience that certain names become associated with certain notions and sentiments, which determine a person's attitude towards men and things. The names, Brahmin, Kshatriya, Vaishya and Shudra, are names which are associated with a definite and fixed notion in the mind of every Hindu. That notion is that of a hierarchy based on birth. So long as these names continue, Hindus will continue to think of the Brahmin, Kshatriya, Vaishya and Shudra as hierarchical divisions of high and low, based on birth, and act accordingly. The Hindu must be made to unlearn all this. But how can this happen if the old labels remain and continue to recall to his mind old notions. If new notions are to be inculcated in the minds of people it is necessary to give them new names. To continue the old name is to make the reform futile. To allow this Chaturvarnya, based on worth to be designated by such stinking labels of Brahmin, Kshatriya, Vaishya, Shudra, indicative of social divisions based on birth, is a snare.

## XVI

To me this Chaturvarnya with its old labels is utterly repellent and my whole being rebels against it. But I do not wish to rest my objection to Chaturvarnya on mere grounds of sentiments. There are more solid grounds on which I rely for my opposition to it. A close examination of this ideal has convinced me that as a system of social organization, Chaturvarnya is impracticable, harmful and has turned out to be a miserable failure. From a practical point of view, the system of Chaturvarnya raises several difficulties which its protagonists do not seem to have taken into account. The principle underlying caste is fundamentally different from the principle underlying *Varna*. Not only are they fundamentally different but they are also fundamentally opposed. The former is based on worth. How are you going to compel people who have acquired a higher status based on birth without reference to their worth to vacate that status ? How are you going to compel people to recognize the status due to a man in accordance with his worth, who is occupying a lower status based on his birth ? For this you must first break up the Caste System, in order to be able to establish the *Varna* system. How are you going to reduce the four thousand castes, based on birth, to the four *Varnas,* based on worth ? This is the first difficulty which the protagonists of the Chaturvarnya must grapple with. There is a second difficulty which the protagonists of Chaturvarnya must grapple with, if they wish to make the establishment of Chaturvarnya a success.

Chaturvarnya pre-supposes that you can classify people into four definite classes. Is this possible ? In this respect, the ideal of Chaturvarnya has, as you will see, a close affinity to the Platonic ideal. To Plato, men fell by nature into three classes. In some individuals, he believed mere appetites dominated. He assigned them to the labouring and trading classes. Others revealed to him that over and above appetites, they have a courageous disposition. He classed them as defenders in war and guardians of internal peace. Others showed a capacity to grasp the universal reason underlying things. He made them the law-givers of the people. The criticism to which Plato's Republic is subject, is also the criticism which must apply to the system of Chaturvarnya, in so far as it proceeds upon the possibility of an accurate classification of men into four distinct classes. The chief criticism against Plato is that his idea of lumping of individuals into a few sharply marked-off classes is a very superficial view of man and his powers. Plato had no perception of the uniqueness of every individual, of his incommensurability with others, of each individual forming a class of his own. He had no recognition of the infinite diversity of active tendencies and combination of tendencies of which an individual is capable. To him, there were types of faculties or powers in the individual constitution. All this is demonstrably wrong. Modern science has shown that lumping together of individuals into a few sharply marked-off classes is a superficial view of man not worthy of serious consideration. Consequently, the utilization of the qualities of individuals is incompitable with their startification by classes, since the qualities of individuals are so variable. Chaturvarnya must fail for the very reason for which Plato's Republic must fail, namely that it is not possible to pigeon men into holes, according as he belongs to one class or the other. That it is impossible to accurately classify people into four definite classes is proved by the fact that the original four classes have now become four thousand castes.

There is a third difficulty in the way of the establishment of the system of Chaturvarnya. How are you going to maintain the system of Chaturvarnya, supposing it was established ? One important requirement for the successful working of Chaturvarnya is the maintenance of the penal system which could maintain it by its sanction. The system of Chaturvarnya must perpetually face the problem of the transgressor. Unless there is a penalty attached to the act of transgression, men will not keep to their respective classes. The whole system will break down, being contrary to human nature. Chaturvarnya cannot subsist by its own inherent goodness. It must be enforced by law.

That, without penal sanction the ideal of Chaturvarnya cannot be realized, is proved by the story in the Ramayana of Rama killing Shambuka. Some people seem to blame Rama because he want only and without reason killed Shambuka. But to blame Rama for killing Shambuka is to misunderstand the whole situation. Ram Raj was a Raj based on Chaturvarnya. As a king, Rama was bound to maintain Chaturvarnya. It was his duty therefore to kill Shambuka, the Shudra, who had transgressed his class and wanted to be a Brahmin. This is the reason why Rama killed Shambuka. But this also shows that penal sanction is necessary for the maintenance of Chaturvarnya. Not only penal sanction is necessary, but penalty of death is necessary. That is why Rama did not inflict on Shambuka a lesser punishment. That is why Manu-Smriti prescribes such heavy sentences as cutting off the tongue or pouring of molten lead in the ears of the Shudra, who recites or hears the *Veda*. The supporters of Chaturvarnya must give an assurance that they could successfully classify men and they could induce modern society in the twentieth century to reforge the penal sanctions of Manu-Smriti.

The protagonists of Chaturvarnya do not seem to have considered what is to happen to women in their system. Are they also to be divided into four classes, Brahmin, Kshatriya, Vaishya and Shudra? Or are they to be allowed to take the status of their husbands. If the status of the woman is to be the consequence of marriage what becomes of the underlying principle of Chaturvarnya, namely, that the status of a person should be based upon the worth of that person? If they are to be classified according to their worth is their classification to be nominal or real? If it is to be nominal then it is useless and then the protagonists of Chaturvarnya must admit that their system does not apply to women. If it is real, are the protagonists of Chaturvarnya prepared to follow the logical consequences of applying it to women? They must be prepared to have women priests and women soldiers. Hindu society has grown accustomed to women teachers and women barristers. It may grow accustomed to women brewers and women butchers. But he would be a bold person, who would say that it will allow women priests and women soldiers. But that will be the logical outcome of applying Chaturvarnya to women. Given these difficulties, I think no one except a congenital idiot could hope and believe in a successful regeneration of the Chaturvarnya.

## XVII

Assuming that Chaturvarnya is practicable, I contend that it is the most vicious system. That the Brahmins should cultivate knowledge, that the Kshatriya should bear arms, that the Vaishya should trade and that the Shudra should serve sounds as though it was a system of division of labour. Whether the theory was intended to state that the Shudra *need not* or that whether it was intended to lay down that he *must not,* is an interesting question. The defenders of Chaturvarnya give it the first meaning. They say, why should the Shudra need trouble to acquire wealth, when the three *Varnas* are there to support him? Why need the Shudra bother to take to education, when there is the Brahmin to whom he can go when the occasion for reading or writing arises? Why need the Shudra worry to arm himself because there is the Kshatriya to protect him? The theory of Chaturvarnya, understood in this sense, may be said to look upon the Shudra as the ward and the three *Varnas* as his guardians. Thus interpreted, it is a simple, elevating and alluring theory. Assuming this to be the correct view of the underlying conception of Chaturvarnya, it seems to me that the system is neither fool-proof nor knave-proof. What is to happen, if the Brahmins, Vaishyas and Kshatriyas fail to pursue knowledge, to engage in economic enterprise and to be efficient soldiers which are their respective functions? Contrary-wise, suppose that they discharge their functions but flout their duty to the Shudra or to one another, what is to happen to the Shudra if the three classes refuse to support him on fair terms or combine to keep him down? Who is to safeguard the interests of the Shudra or for the matter of that of the Vaishya and Kshatriya when the person, who is trying to take advantage of his ignorance is the Brahmin? Who is to defend the liberty of the Shudra and for the matter of that, of the Brahmin and the Vaishya when the person who is robbing him of it is the Kshatriya? Inter-dependence of one class on another class is inevitable. Even dependence of one class upon another may sometimes become allowable. But why make one person depend upon another in the matter of his vital needs? Education everyone must have. Means of defence everyone must have. These are the paramount requirements of every man for his self-preservation. How can the fact that his neighbour is educated and armed help a man who is uneducated and disarmed. The whole theory is absurd. These are the questions, which the defenders of Chaturvarnya do not seem to be troubled about. But they are very pertinent questions. Assuming their conception of Chaturvarnya that the relationship between the different classes is that of ward and guardian is the real conception underlying Chaturvarnya, it must be admitted that it makes no provision to safeguard the interests of the ward from the misdeeds of the guardian. Whether the relationship of guardian and ward was the real underlying conception, on which Chaturvarnya was based, there is no doubt that in practice the relation was that of master and servants. The three classes, Brahmins, Kshatriyas and Vaishyas although not very happy in their mutual relationship managed to work by compromise. The Brahmin flattered the Kshatriya and both let the Vaishya live in order to be able to live upon him. But the three agreed to beat down the Shudra. He was not allowed to acquire wealth lest he should be independent of the three *Varnas*. He was prohibited from acquiring knowledge lest he should keep a steady vigil regarding his interests. He was prohibited from bearing arms lest he should have the means to rebel against their authority. That this is how the Shudras were treated by the Tryavarnikas is evidenced by the Laws of Manu. There is no code of laws more in famous regarding social rights than the Laws of Manu. Any instance from anywhere of social injustice must pale before it. Why have the mass of people tolerated the social evils to which they have been subjected ? There have been social revolutions in other countries of the world. Why have there not been social revolutions in India, is a question which has incessantly troubled me. There is only one answer, which I can give and it is that the lower classes of Hindus have been completely disabled for direct action on account of this wretched system of Chaturvarnya. They could not bear arms and without arms they could not rebel. They were all ploughmen or rather condemned to be ploughmen and they never were allowed to convert their ploughshare into swords. They had no bayonets and therefore everyone who chose could and did sit upon them. On account of the Chaturvarnya, they could receive no education. They could not think out or know the way to their salvation. They were condemned to be lowly and not knowing the way of escape and not having the means of escape, they became reconciled to eternal servitude, which they accepted as their inescapable fate. It is true that even in Europe the strong has not shrunk from the exploitation, nay the spoliation of the weak. But in Europe, the strong have never contrived to make the weak helpless against exploitation so shamelessly as was the case in India among the Hindus. Social war has been raging between the strong and the weak far more violently in Europe than it has ever been in India. Yet, the weak in Europe has had in his freedom of military service his *physical weapon,* in suffering his *political weapon* and in education his *moral weapon.* These three weapons for emancipation were never withheld by the strong from the weak in Europe. All these weapons were, however, denied to the masses in India by Chaturvarnya. There cannot be a more degrading system of social organization than the Chaturvarnya. It is the system which deadens, paralyses and cripples the people from helpful activity. This is no exaggeration. History bears ample evidence. There is only one period in Indian history which is a period of freedom, greatness and glory. That is the period of the Mourya Empire. At all other times the country suffered from defeat and darkness. But the Mourya period was a period when Chaturvarnya was completely annihilated, when the Shudras, who constituted the mass of the people, came into their own and became the rulers of the country. The period of defeat and darkness is the period when Chaturvarnya flourished to the damnation of the greater part of the people of the country.

## XVIII

Chaturvarnya is not new. It is as old as the *Vedas.* That is one of the reasons why we are asked by the Arya Samajists to consider its claims. Judging from the past as a system of social organization, it has been tried and it has failed. How many times have the Brahmins annihilated the seed of the Kshatriyas ! How many times have the Kshatriyas annihilated the Brahmins! The Mahabharata and the Puranas are full of incidents of the strife between the Brahmins and the Kshatriyas. They even quarreled over such petty questions as to who should salute first, as to who should give way first, the Brahmins or the Kshatriyas, when the two met in the street. Not only was the Brahmin an eyesore to the Kshatriya and the Kshatriya an eyesore to the Brahmin, it seems that the Kshatriyas had become tyrannical and the masses, disarmed as they were under the system of Chaturvarnya, were praying Almighty God for relief from their tyranny. The Bhagwat tells us very definitely that Krishna had taken Avtar for one sacred purpose and that was to annihilate the Kshatriyas. With these instances of rivalry and enmity between the different *Varnas* before us, I do not understand how any one can hold out Chaturvarnya as an ideal to be aimed at or as a pattern, on which the Hindu Society should be remodelled,

## XIX

I have dealt with those, who are without you and whose hostility to your ideal is quite open. There appear to be others, who are neither without you not with you. I was hesitating whether I should deal with their point of view. But on further consideration I have come to the conclusion that I must and that for two reasons. Firstly, their attitude to the problem of caste is not merely an attitude of neutrality, but is an attitude of armed neutrality. Secondly, they probably represent a considerable body of people. Of these, there is one set which finds nothing peculiar nor odious in the Caste System of the Hindus. Such Hindus cite the case of Muslims, Sikhs and Christians and find comfort in the fact that they too have castes amongst them. In considering, this question you must at the outset bear in mind that nowhere is human society one single whole. It is always plural. In the world of action, the individual is one limit and society the other. Between them lie all sorts of associative arrangements of lesser and larger scope, families, friendship, co-operative associations, business combines, political parties, bands of thieves and robbers. These small groups are usually firmly welded together and are often as exclusive as castes. They have a narrow and intensive code, which is often anti-social. This is true of every society, in Europe as well as in Asia. The question to be asked in determining whether a given society is an ideal society; is not whether there are groups in it, because groups exist in all societies. The questions to be asked in determining what is an ideal society are : How numerous and varied are the interests which are consciously shared by the groups ? How full and free is the interplay with other forms of associations ? Are the forces that separate groups and classes more numerous than the forces that unite ? What social significance is attached to this group life ? Is its exclusiveness a matter of custom and convenience or is it a matter of religion ? It is in the light of these questions that one must decide whether caste among Non-Hindus is the same as caste among Hindus. If we apply these considerations to castes among Mohammedans, Sikhs and Christians on the one hand and to castes among Hindus on the other, you will find that caste among Non-Hindus is fundamentally different from caste among Hindus. First, the ties, which consciously make the Hindus hold together, are non-existent, while among Non-Hindus there are many that hold them together. The strength of a society depends upon the presence of points of contact, possibilities of interaction between different groups which exist in it. These are what Carlyle calls "organic filaments" *i.e.* the elastic threads which help to bring the disintegrating elements together and to reunite them. There is no integrating force among the Hindus to counteract the disintegration caused by caste. While among the Non-Hindus there are plenty of these organic filaments which bind them together. Again it must be borne in mind that although there are castes among Non-Hindus, as there are among Hindus, caste has not the same social significance for Non-Hindus as it has for Hindus. Ask Mohammedan or a Sikh, who he is? He tells you that he is a Mohammedan or a Sikh as the case may be. He does not tell you his caste although he has one and you are satisfied with his answer. When he tells you that he is a Muslim, you do not proceed to ask him whether he is a Shiya or a Sunni; Sheikh or Saiyad; Khatik or Pinjari. When he tells you he is a Sikh, you do not ask him whether he is Jat or Roda; Mazbi or Ramdasi. But you are not satisfied, if a person tells you that he is a Hindu. You feel bound to inquire into his caste. Why? Because so essential is caste in the case of a Hindu that without knowing it you do not feel sure what sort of a being he is. That caste has not the same social significance among Non-Hindus as it has among Hindus is clear if you take into consideration the consequences which follow breach of caste. There may be castes among Sikhs and Mohammedans but the Sikhs and the Mohammedans will not outcast a Sikh or a Mohammedan if he broke his caste. Indeed, the very idea of excommunication is foreign to the Sikhs and the Mohammedans. But with the Hindus the case is entirely different. He is sure to be outcasted if he broke caste. This shows the difference in the social significance of caste to Hindus and Non-Hindus. This is the second point of difference. But there is also a third and a more important one. Caste among the non-Hindus has no religious consecration; but among the Hindus most decidedly it has. Among the Non-Hindus, caste is only a practice, not a sacred institution. They, did not originate it. With them it is only a survival. They do not regard caste as a religious dogma. Religion compels the Hindus to treat isolation and segregation of castes as a virtue. Religion does not compel the Non-Hindus to take the same attitude towards caste. If Hindus wish to break caste, their religion will come in their way. But it will not be so in the case of Non-Hindus. It is, therefore, a dangerous delusion to take comfort in the mere existence of caste among Non-Hindus, without caring to know what place caste occupies in their life and whether there are other "organic filaments", which subordinate the feeling of caste to the feeling of community. The sooner the Hindus are cured of this delusion the better.

The other set denies that caste presents any problem at all for the Hindus to consider. Such Hindus seek comfort in the view that the Hindus have survived and take this as a proof of their fitness to survive. This point of view is well expressed by Prof. S. Radhakrishnan in his *Hindu view of Life*. Referring to Hinduism he says, "The civilization itself has not been a shortlived one. Its historic records date back for over four thousand years and even then it had reached a stage of civilization which has continued its unbroken, though at times slow and static, course until the present day. It has stood the stress and strain of more than four or five millenniums of spiritual thought and experience. Though peoples of different races and cultures have been pouring into India from the dawn of History, Hinduism has been able to maintain its supremacy and even the proselytising creeds backed by political power have not been able to coerce the large majority of Hindus to their views. The Hindu culture possesses some vitality which seems to be denied to some other more forceful currents. It is no more necessary to dissect Hinduism than to open a tree to see whether the sap still runs." The name of Prof. Radhakrishnan is big enough to invest with profundity whatever he says and impress the minds of his readers. But I must not hesitate to speak out my mind. For, I fear that, his statement may become the basis of a vicious argument that the fact of survival is proof of fitness to survive. It seems to me that the question is not whether a community lives or dies; the question is on what plane does it live. There are different modes of survival. But all are not equally honourable. For an individual as well as for a society, there is a gulf between merely living and living worthily. To fight in a battle and to live in glory is one mode. To beat a retreat, to surrender and to live the life of a captive is also a mode of survival. It is useless for a Hindu to take comfort in the fact that he and his people have survived. What he must consider is what is the quality of their survival. If he does that, I am sure he will cease to take pride in the mere fact of survival. A Hindu's life has been a life of continuous defeat and what appears to him to be life everlasting is not living everlastingly but is really a life which is perishing everlastingly. It is a mode of survival of which every right-minded Hindu, who is not afraid to own up the truth, will feel ashamed.

## XX

There is no doubt, in my opinion, that unless you change your social order you can achieve little by way of progress. You cannot mobilize the community either for defence or for offence. You cannot build anything on the foundations of caste. You cannot build up a nation, you cannot build up a morality. Anything that you will build on the foundations of caste will crack and will never be a whole.

The only question that remains to be considered is—*How to bring about the reform of the Hindu social order? How to abolish caste?* This is a question of supreme importance. There is a view that in the reform of caste, the first step to take, is to abolish sub-castes. This view is based upon the supposition that there is a greater similarity in manners and status between sub-castes than there is between castes. I think, this is an erroneous supposition. The Brahmins of Northern and Central India are socially of lower grade, as compared with the Brahmins of the Deccan and Southern India. The former are only cooks and water-carriers while the latter occupy a high social position. On the other hand, in Northern India, the Vaishyas and Kayasthas are intellectually and socially on a par with the Brahmins of the Deccan and Southern India. Again, in the matter of food there is no similarity between the Brahmins of the Deccan and Southern India, who are vegetarians and the Brahmins of Kashmir and Bengal who are non-vegetarians. On the other hand, the Brahmins of the Deccan and Southern India have more in common so far as food is concerned with such non-Brahmins as the Gujaratis, Marwaris, Banias and Jains. There is no doubt that from the standpoint of making the transit from one caste to another easy, the fusion of the Kayasthas of Northern India and the other Non-Brahmins of Southern India with the Non-Brahmins of the Deccan and the Dravid country is more practicable than the fusion of the Brahmins of the South with the Brahmins of the North. But assuming that the fusion of sub-Castes is possible, what guarantee is there that the abolition of sub-Castes will necessarily lead to the abolition of Castes? On the contrary, it may happen that the process may stop with the abolition of sub-Castes. In that case, the abolition of sub-Castes will only help to strengthen the Castes and make them more powerful and therefore more mischievous. This remedy is therefore neither practicable nor effective and may easily prove to be a wrong remedy. Another plan of action for the abolition of Caste is to begin with inter-caste dinners. This also, in my opinion, is an inadequate remedy. There are many Castes which allow inter-dining. But it is a common experience that inter-dining has not succeeded in killing the spirit of Caste and the consciousness of Caste. I am convinced that the real remedy is inter-marriage. Fusion of blood can alone create the feeling of being kith and kin and unless this feeling of kinship, of being kindred, becomes paramount the separatist feeling—the feeling of being aliens— created by Caste will not vanish. Among the Hindus inter-marriage must necessarily be a factor of greater force in social life than it need be in the life of the non-Hindus. Where society is already well-knit by other ties, marriage is an ordinary incident of life. But where society cut asunder, marriage as a binding force becomes a matter of urgent necessity. *The real remedy for breaking Caste is inter-marriage. Nothing else will serve as the solvent of Caste.* Your Jat-Pat-Todak Mandal has adopted this line of attack

It is a direct, and frontal attack, and I congratulate you upon a correct diagnosis and more upon your having shown the courage to tell the Hindus what is really wrong with them. Political tyranny is nothing compared to social tyranny and a reformer, who defies society, is a much more courageous man than a politician, who defies Government. You are right in holding that Caste will cease to be an operative force only when inter-dining and inter-marriage have become matters of common course. You have located the source of the disease. But is your prescription the right prescription for the disease ? Ask yourselves this question; Why is it that a large majority of Hindus do not inter-dine and do not inter-marry? Why is it that your cause is not popular ? There can be only one answer to this question and it is that inter-dining and inter-marriage are repugnant to the beliefs and dogmas which the Hindus regard as sacred. Caste is not a physical object like a wall of bricks or a line of barbed wire which prevents the Hindus from co-mingling and which has, therefore, to be pulled down. Caste is a notion, it is a state of the mind. The destruction of Caste does not therefore mean the destruction of a physical barrier. It means a *notional* change. Caste may be bad. Caste may lead to conduct so gross as to be called man's inhumanity to man. All the same, it must be recognized that the Hindus observe Caste not because they are inhuman or wrong headed. They observe Caste because they are deeply religious. People are not wrong in observing Caste. In my view, what is wrong is their religion, which has inculcated this notion of Caste. If this is correct, then obviously the enemy, you must grapple with, is not the people who observe Caste, but the *Shastras* which teach them this religion of Caste. Criticising and ridiculing people for not inter-dining or inter-marrying or occasionally holding inter-caste dinners and celebrating inter-caste marriages, is a futile method of achieving the desired end. The real remedy is to destroy the belief in the sanctity of the *Shastras*. How do you expect to succeed, if you allow the *Shastras* to continue to mould the beliefs and opinions of the people ? Not to question the authority of the *Shastras,* to permit the people to believe in their sanctity and their sanctions and to blame them and to criticise them for their acts as being irrational and inhuman is a incongruous way of carrying on social reform. Reformers working for the removal of untouchability including Mahatma Gandhi, do not seem to realize that the acts of the people are merely the results of their beliefs inculcated upon their minds by the *Shastras* and that people will not change their conduct until they cease to believe in the sanctity of the *Shastras* on which their conduct is founded. No wonder that such efforts have not produced any results. You also seem to be erring in the same way as the reformers working in the cause of removing untouchability. To agitate for and to organise inter-caste dinners and inter-caste marriages is like forced feeding brought about by artificial means. Make every man and woman free from the thraldom of the *Shastras,* cleanse their minds of the pernicious notions founded on the *Shastras,* and he or she will inter-dine and inter-marry, without your telling him or her to do so.

It is no use seeking refuge in quibbles. It is no use telling people that the *Shastras* do not say what they are believed to say, grammatically read or logically interpreted. What matters is how the *Shastras* have been understood by the people. You must take the stand that Buddha took. You must take the stand which Guru Nanak took. You must not only discard the *Shastras,* you must deny their authority, as did Buddha and Nanak. You must have courage to tell the Hindus, that what is wrong with them is their religion—the religion which has produced in them this notion of the sacredness of Caste. Will you show that courage?

## XXI

What are your chances of success? Social reforms fall into different species. There is a species of reform, which does not relate to the religious notion of people but is purely secular in character. There is also a species of reform, which relates to the religious notions of people. Of such a species of reform, there are two varieties. In one, the reform accords with the principles of the religion and merely invites people, who have departed from it, to revert to them and to follow them. The second is a reform which not only touches the religious principles but is diametrically opposed to those principles and invites people to depart from and to discard their authority and to act contrary to those principles. Caste is the natural outcome of certain religious beliefs which have the sanction of the *Shastras,* which are believed to contain the command of divinely inspired sages who were endowed with a supernatural wisdom and whose commands, therefore, cannot be disobeyed without committing sin. The destruction of Caste is a reform which falls under the third category. To ask people to give up Caste is to ask them to go contrary to their fundamental religious notions. It is obvious that the first and second species of reform are easy. But the third is a stupendous task, well-nigh impossible. The Hindus hold to the sacredness of the social order. Caste has a divine basis. You must therefore destroy the sacredness and divinity with which Caste has become invested. In the last analysis, this means you must destroy the authority of the *Shastras* and the *Vedas.*

I have emphasized this question of the ways and means of destroying Caste, because I think that knowing the proper ways and means is more important than knowing the ideal. If you do not know the real ways and means, all your shots are sure to be misfires. If my analysis is correct then your task is herculean. You alone can say whether you are capable of achieving it.

Speaking for myself, I see the task to be well-nigh impossible. Perhaps you would like to know why I think so. Out of the many reasons, which have led me to take this view, I will mention some, which I regard much important.

One of these reasons is the attitude of hostility, which the Brahmins have shown towards this question. The Brahmins form the vanguard of the movement for political reform and in some cases also of economic reform. But they are not to be found even as camp-followers in the army raised to break down the barricades of Caste. Is there any hope of the Brahmins ever taking up a lead in the future in this matter ? I say no. You may ask why ? You may argue that there is no reason why Brahmins should continue to shun social reform. You may argue that the Brahmins know that the bane of Hindu Society is Caste and as an enlightened class could not be expected to be indifferent to its consequences. You may argue that there are secular Brahmins and priestly Brahmins and if the latter do not take up the cudgels on behalf of those who want to break Caste, the former will. All this of course sounds very plausible. But in all this it is forgotten that the break up of the Caste system is bound to affect adversely the Brahmin Caste. Having regard to this, is it reasonable to expect that the Brahmins will ever consent to lead a movement the ultimate result of which is to destroy the power and prestige of the Brahmin Caste ? Is it reasonable to expect the secular Brahmins to take part in a movement directed against the priestly Brahmins ? In my judgment, it is useless to make a distinction between the secular Brahmins and priestly Brahmins. Both are kith and kin. They are two arms of the same body and one bound to fight for the existence of the other. In this connection, I am reminded of some very pregnant remarks made by Prof. Dicey in his *English Constitution.* Speaking of the actual limitation on the legislative supremacy of Parliament, Dicey says : "The actual exercise of authority by any sovereign whatever, and notably by Parliament, is bounded or controlled by two limitations. Of these the one is an external, and the other is an internal limitation. The external limit to the real power of a sovereign consists in the possibility or certainty that his subjects or a large number of them will disobey or resist his laws. . . The internal limit to the exercise of sovereignty arises from the nature of the sovereign power itself. Even a despot exercises his powers in accordance with his character, which is itself moulded by the circumstance under which he lives, including under that head the moral feelings of the time and the society to which he belongs. The Sultan could not, if he would, change the religion of the Mohammedan world, but even if he could do so, it is in the very highest degree improbable that the head of Mohammedanism should wish to overthrow the religion of Mohammed ; the internal check on the exercise of the Sultan's power is at least as strong as the external limitation. People sometimes ask the idle question, why the Pope does not introduce this or that reform ? The true answer is that a revolutionist is not the kind of man who becomes a Pope and that a man who becomes a Pope has no wish to be a revolutionist." I think, these remarks apply equally to the Brahmins of India and one can say with equal truth that if a man who becomes a Pope has no wish to become a revolutionary, a man who is born a Brahmin has much less desire to become a revolutionary. Indeed, to expect a Brahmin to be a revolutionary in matters of social reform is as idle as to expect the British Parliament, as was said by Leslie Stephen, to pass an Act requiring all blue-eyed babies to be murdered.

Some of you will say that it is a matter of small concern whether the Brahmins come forward to lead the movement against Caste or whether they do not. To take this view is in my judgment to ignore the part played by the intellectual class in the community. Whether you accept the theory of the great man as the maker of history or whether you do not, this much you will have to concede that in every country the intellectual class is the most influential class, if not the governing class. The intellectual class is the class which can foresee, it is the class which can advise and give lead. In no country does the mass of the people live the life of intelligent thought and action. It is largely imitative and follows the intellectual class. There is no exaggeration in saying that the entire destiny of a country depends upon its intellectual class. If the intellectual class is honest, independent and disinterested it can be trusted to take the initiative and give a proper lead when a crisis arises. It is true that intellect by itself is no virtue. It is only a means and the use of means depends upon the ends which an intellectual person pursues. An intellectual man can be a good man but he can easily be a rogue. Similarly an intellectual class may be a band of high-souled persons, ready to help, ready to emancipate erring humanity or it may easily be a gang of crooks or a body of advocates of a narrow clique from which it draws its support. You may think it a pity that the intellectual class in India is simply another name for the Brahmin caste. You may regret that the two are one ; that the existence of the intellectual class should be bound with one single caste, that this intellectual class should share the interest and the aspirations of that Brahmin caste, which has regarded itself the custodian of the interest of that caste, rather than of the interests of the country. All this may be very regrettable. But the fact remains, that the Brahmins form the intellectual class of the Hindus. It is not only an intellectual class but it is a class which is held in great reverence by the rest of the Hindus. The Hindus are taught that the Brahmins are *Bhudevas* (Gods on earth) वर्णानाम् ब्राह्मण । गुरु; The Hindus are taught that Brahmins alone can be their teachers. Manu says, "If it be asked how it should be with respect to points of the Dharma which have not been specially mentioned, the answer is that which Brahmins who are Shishthas propound shall doubtless have legal force." :

अनाम्नातेषु धर्मेषु कथं स्यादिति चेद्भवेत् ।
यं शिष्टा ब्राह्मणा ब्रूयुः स धर्मः स्यादशङ्कितः ।

When such an intellectual class, which holds the rest of the community in its grip, is opposed to the reform of Caste, the chances of success in a movement for the break-up of the Caste system appear to me very, very remote.

The second reason, why I say the task is impossible, will be clear if you will bear in mind that the Caste system has two aspects. In one of its aspects, it divides men into separate communities. In its second aspect, it places these communities in a graded order one above the other in social status. Each caste takes its pride and its consolation in the fact that in the scale of castes it is above some other caste. As an outward mark of this gradation, there is also a gradation of social and religious rights technically spoken of an *Ashta-dhikaras* and *Sanskaras*. The higher the grade of a caste, the greater the number of these rights and the lower the grade, the lesser their number. Now this gradation, this scaling of castes, makes it impossible to organise a common front against the Caste System. If a caste claims the right to inter-dine and inter-marry with another caste placed above it, it is frozen, instantly it is told by mischief-mongers, and there are many Brahmins amongst such mischief-mongers, that it will have to concede inter-dining and inter-marriage with castes below it! All are slaves of the Caste System. But all the slaves are not equal in status. To excite the proletariat to bring about an economic revolution, Karl Marx told them: "You have nothing to lose except your chains." But the artful way in which the social and religious rights are distributed among the different castes whereby some have more and some have less, makes the slogan of Karl Marx quite useless to excite the Hindus against the Caste System. Castes form a graded system of sovereignties, high and low, which are jealous of their status and which know that if a general dissolution came, some of them stand to lose more of their prestige and power than others do. You cannot, therefore, have a general mobilization of the Hindus, to use a military expression, for an attack on the Caste System.

## XXII

Can you appeal to reason and ask the Hindus to discard Caste as being contrary to reason? That raises the question: Is a Hindu free to follow his reason? Manu has laid down three sanctions to which every Hindu must conform in the matter of his behaviour वेद: स्मृति: सदाचार: स्वस्य च प्रियमात्मन: Here there is no place for reason to play its part. A Hindu must follow either *Veda, Smriti* or *Sadachar*. He cannot follow anything else. In the first place how are the texts of the *Vedas* and *Smritis* to be interpreted whenever any doubt arises regarding their meaning? On this important question the view of Manu is quite definite. He says:

योऽवमन्येत ते मूले हेतुशास्त्राश्रयात् द्विज: ।
स साधुभिर्बहिष्कार्यो नास्तिको वेदनिन्दक: ॥

According to this rule, rationalism as a canon of interpreting the *Vedas* and *Smritis,* is absolutely condemned. It is regarded to be as wicked as atheism and the punishment provided for it is ex-communication. Thus, where a matter is covered by the *Veda* or the *Smriti,* a Hindu cannot resort to rational thinking. Even when there is a conflict between *Vedas* and *Smritis* on matters on which they have given a positive injunction, the solution is not left to reason. When there is a conflict between two *Shrutis,* both are to be regarded as of equal authority. Either of them may be followed. No attempt is to be made to find out which of the two accords with reason. This is made clear by *Manu* :

श्रुतिद्वैधं तु यत्र स्याप्तत्र धर्मावुभौ स्मृतौ ।

"When there is a conflict between *Shruti* and *Smriti,* the *Shruti* must prevail." But here too, no attempt must be made to find out which of the two accords with reason. This is laid down by Manu in the following Shloka :

या वेदबाह्या: स्मृतयो याश्च काश्च कुदृष्ट: ।
सर्वास्ता निष्फला: प्रेत्य तमोनिष्ठा हि त: स्मृता: ॥

Again, when there is a conflict between two *Smritis,* the Manu-Smriti must prevail, but no attempt is to be made to find out which of the two accords with reason. This is the ruling given by Brihaspati:

वेदायत्वोपनिबंधृत्वत् प्रमाण्यं हि मनो: स्मृतं ।
मन्वर्थविपरीता तु या स्मृति: सा न शस्यते ॥

It is, therefore, clear that in any matter on which the *Shrutis* and *Smritis* have given a positive direction, a Hindu is not free to use his reasoning faculty. The same rule is laid down in the Mahabharat:

पुराणं मानवो धर्म: सांगो वेदश्चिकित्सितं ।
आज्ञासिद्धानि चत्वारि न हन्तव्यानि हेतुभि: ॥

He must abide by their directions. The Caste and *Varna* are matters, which are dealt with by the *Vedas* and the *Smritis* and consequently, appeal to reason can have no effect on a Hindu. So far as Caste and *Varna* are concerned, not only the *Shastras* do not permit the Hindu to use his reason in the decision of the question, but they have taken care to see that no occasion is left to examine in a rational way the foundations of his belief in Caste and *Varna*. It must be a source of silent amusement to many a Non-Hindu to find hundreds and thousands of Hindus breaking Caste on certain occasions, such as railway journey and foreign travel and yet endeavouring to maintain Caste for the rest of their lives! The explanation of this phenomenon discloses another fetter on the reasoning faculties of the Hindus. Man's life is generally habitual and unreflective. Reflective thought, in the sense of active, persistent and careful consideration of any belief or supposed form or knowledge in the light of the grounds that support it and further conclusions to which it tends, is quite rare and arises only in a situation which presents a dilemma—a crisis. Railway journeys and foreign travels are really occasions of crisis in the life of a Hindu and it is natural to expect a Hindu to ask himself why he should maintain Caste at all, if he cannot maintain it at all times. But he does not. He breaks Caste at one step and proceeds to observe it at the next without raising any question. The reason for this astonishing conduct is to be found in the rule of the *Shastras,* which directs him to maintain Caste as far as possible and to undergo *prayaschitta* when he cannot. By this theory of *prayaschitta,* the *Shastras* by following a spirit of compromise have given caste a perpetual lease of life and have smothered reflective thought which would have otherwise led to the destruction of the notion of Caste.

There have been many who have worked in the cause of the abolition of Caste and Untouchability. Of those, who can be mentioned, Ramanuja, Kabir and others stand out prominently. Can you appeal to the acts of these reformers and exhort the Hindus to follow them ? It is true that Manu has included *Sadachar* (सदाचार) as one of the sanctions along with *Shruti* and *Smriti.* Indeed, *Sadachar* has been given a higher place than *Shastras :*

यद्यद्याचर्यते येन धर्म्यं वाऽधर्म्यमेव वा ।
देशस्याचरणं नित्यं चरित्रं तद्धिकीर्तितम् ॥

According to this, *Sadachar,* whether, it is धर्म्य or अधर्म्य in accordance with *Shastras* or contrary to *Shastras,* must be followed. But what is the meaning of *Sadachar* ? If any one were to suppose that *Sadachar* means right or good acts *i.e.* acts of good and righteous men he would find himself greatly mistaken. *Sadachar* does not means good acts or acts of good men. It means ancient custom *good* or *bad.* The following verse makes this clear :

यस्मिन् देशे य आचार: पारंपर्यक्रमागत: ।
वर्णानां किल सर्वेषां स सदाचार उच्यते ॥

As though to warn people against the view that *Sadachar* means good acts or acts of good men and fearing that people might understand it that way and follow the acts of good men, the *Smritis* have commanded the Hindus in unmistakable terms not to follow even Gods in their good deeds, if they are contrary to *Shruti, Smriti* and *Sadachar.* This may sound to be most extraordinary, most perverse, but the fact remains that न देवचरितं चरेत् is an injunction, issued to the Hindus by their *Shastras.* Reason and morality are the two most powerful weapons in the armoury of a Reformer. To deprive him of the use of these weapons is to disable him for action. How are you going to break up Caste, if people are not free to consider whether it accords with reason ? How are you going to break up Caste it people are not free to consider whether it accords with morality ? The wall built around Caste is impregnable and the material, of which it is built, contains none of the combustible stuff of reason and morality. Add to this the fact that inside this wall stands the army of Brahmins who form the intellectual class, Brahmins who are the natural leaders of the Hindus, Brahmins who are there not as mere mercenary soldiers but as an army fighting for its homeland and you will get an idea why I think that breaking-up of Caste amongst the Hindus is well-nigh impossible. At any rate, it would take ages before a breach is made. But whether the doing of the deed takes time or whether it can be done quickly, you must not forget that if you wish to bring about a breach in the system then you have got to apply the dynamite to the *Vedas* and the *Shastras,* which deny any part to reason, to *Vedas* and *Shastras,* which deny any part to morality. You must destroy the Religion of the *Shrutis* and the *Smritis.* Nothing else will avail. This is my considered view of the matter.

## XXIII

Some may not understand what I mean by destruction of Religion ; some may find the idea revolting to them and some may find it revolutionary. Let me therefore explain my position. I do not know whether you draw a distinction between principles and rules. But I do. Not only I make a distinction but I say that this distinction is real and important. Rules are practical; they are habitual ways of doing things according to prescription. But principles are intellectual; they are useful methods of judging things. Rules seek to tell an agent just what course of action to pursue. Principles do not prescribe a specific course of action. Rules, like cooking recipes, do tell just what to do and how to do it. A principle, such as that of justice, supplies a main head by reference to which he is to consider the bearings of his desires and purposes, it guides him in his thinking by suggesting to him the important consideration which he should bear in mind. This difference between rules and principles makes the acts done in pursuit of them different in quality and in content. Doing what is said to be good by virtue of a rule and doing good in the light of a principle are two different things. The principle may be wrong but the act is conscious and responsible. The rule may be right but the act is mechanical. A religious act may not be a correct act but must at least be a responsible act. To permit of this responsibility, Religion must mainly be a matter of principles only. It cannot be a matter of rules. The moment it degenerates into rules it ceases to be Religion, as it kills responsibility which is the essence of a truly religious act. What is this Hindu Religion ? Is it a set of principles or is it a code of rules ? Now the Hindu Religion, as contained in the *Vedas* and the *Smritis,* is nothing but a mass of sacrificial, social, political and sanitary rules and regulations, all mixed up. What is called Religion by the Hindus is nothing but a multitude of commands and prohibitions. Religion, in the sense of spiritual principles, truly universal, applicable to all races, to all countries, to all times, is not to be found in them, and if it is, it does not form the governing part of a Hindu's life. That for a Hindu, Dharma means commands and prohibitions is clear from the way the word Dharma is used in *Vedas* and the *Smritis* and understood by the commentators. The word Dharma as used in the *Vedas* in most cases means religious ordinances or rites. Even Jaimini in his Purva-Mimansa defines Dharma as "a desirable goal or result that is indicated by injunctive (*Vedic*) passages". To put it in plain language, what the Hindus call Religion is really Law or at best legalized class-ethics. Frankly, I refuse to call this code of ordinances, as Religion. The first evil of such a code of ordinances, misrepresented to the people as Religion, is that it tends to deprive moral life of freedom and spontaneity and to reduce it (for the conscientious at any rate) to a more or less anxious and servile conformity to externally imposed rules. Under it, there is no loyalty to ideals, there is only conformity to commands. But the worst evil of this code of ordinances is that the laws it contains must be the same yesterday, today and forever. They are iniquitous in that they are not the same for one class as for another. But this iniquity is made perpetual in that they are prescribed to be the same for all generations. The objectionable part of such a scheme is not that they are made by certain persons called Prophets or Law-givers. The objectionable part is that this code has been invested with the character of finality and fixity. Happiness notoriously varies with the conditions and circumstances of a person, as well as with the conditions of different people and epochs. That being the case, how can humanity endure this code of eternal laws, without being cramped and without being crippled ? I have, therefore, no hesitation in saying that such a religion must be destroyed and I say, there is nothing irreligious in working for the destruction of such a religion. Indeed I hold that it is your bounden duty to tear the mask, to remove the misrepresentation that as caused by misnaming this Law as Religion. This is an essential step for you. Once you clear the minds of the people of this misconception and enable them to realize that what they are told as Religion is not Religion but that it is really Law, you will be in a position to urge for its amendment or abolition. So long as people look upon it as Religion they will not be ready for a change, because the idea of Religion is generally speaking not associated with the idea of change. But the idea of law is associated with the idea of change and when people come to know that what is called Religion is really Law, old and archaic, they will be ready for a change, for people know and accept that law can be changed.

## XXIV

While I condemn a Religion of Rules, I must not be understood to hold the opinion that there is no necessity for a religion. On the contrary, I agree with Burke when he says that, "True religion is the foundation of society, the basis on which all true Civil Government rests, and both their sanction." Consequently, when I urge that these ancient rules of life be annulled, I am anxious that its place shall be taken by a Religion of Principles, which alone can lay claim to being a true Religion. Indeed, I am so convinced of the necessity of Religion that I feel I ought to tell you in outline what I regard as necessary items in this religious reform. The following in my opinion should be the cardinal items in this reform : (1) There should be one and only one standard book of Hindu Religion, acceptable to all Hindus and recognized by all Hindus. This of course means that all other books of Hindu religion such as *Vedas, Shastras* and *Puranas,* which are treated as sacred and authoritative, must by law cease to be so and the preaching of any doctrine, religious or social contained in these books should be penalized. (2) It should be better if priesthood among Hindus was abolished. But as this seems to be impossible, the priesthood must at least cease to be hereditary. Every person who professes to be a Hindu must be eligible for being a priest. It should be provided by law that no Hindu shall be entitled to be a priest unless he has passed an examination prescribed by the State and holds a *sanad* from the State permitting him to practise. (3) No ceremony performed by a priest who does not hold a *sanad* shall be deemed to be valid in law and it should be made penal for a person who has no *sanad* to officiate as a priest. (4) A priest should be the servant of the State and should be subject to the disciplinary action by the State in the matter of his morals, beliefs and worship, in addition to his being subject along with other citizens to the ordinary law of the land. (5) The number of priests should be limited by law according to the requirements of the State as is done in the case of the I.C.S. To some, this may sound radical. But to my mind there is nothing revolutionary in this. Every profession in India is regulated. Engineers must show proficiency, Doctor must show proficiency, Lawyers must show proficiency, before they are allowed to practise their professions. During the whole of their career, they must not only obey the law of the land, civil as well as criminal, but they must also obey the special code of morals prescribed by their respective professions. The priest's is the only profession where proficiency is not required. The profession of a Hindu priest is the only profession which is not subject to any code. Mentally a priest may be an idiot, physically a priest may be suffering from a foul disease, such as syphilis or gonorrhea, morally he may be a wreck. But he is fit to officiate at solemn ceremonies, to enter the *sanctum sanctorum* of a Hindu temple and worship the Hindu God. All this becomes possible among the Hindus because for a priest it is enough to be born in a priestly caste. The whole thing is abominable and is due to the fact that the priestly class among Hindus is subject neither to law nor to morality. It recognizes no duties. It knows only of rights and privileges. It is a pest which divinity seems to have let loose on the masses for their mental and moral degradation. The priestly class must be brought under control by some such legislation as I have outlined above. It will prevent it from doing mischief and from misguiding people. It will democratise it by throwing it open to every one. It will certainly help to kill the Brahminism and will also help to kill Caste, which is nothing but Brahminism incarnate. Brahminism is the poison which has spoiled Hinduism. You will succeed in saving Hinduism if you will kill Brahminism. There should be no opposition to this reform from any quarter. It should be welcomed even by the Arya Samajists, because this is merely an application of their own doctrine of *guna-karma*.

Whether you do that or you do not, you must give a new doctrinal basis to your Religion—a basis that will be in consonance with Liberty, Equality and Fraternity, in short, with Democracy. I am no authority on the subject.

But I am told that for such religious principles as will be in consonance with Liberty, Equality and Fraternity it may not be necessary for you to borrow from foreign sources and that you could draw for such principles on the *Upanishads*. Whether you could do so without a complete remoulding, a considerable scraping and chipping off the ore they contain, is more than I can say. This means a complete change in the fundamental notions of life. It means a complete change in the values of life. It means a complete change in outlook and in attitude towards men and things. It means conversion; but if you do not like the word, I will say, it means new life. But a new life cannot enter a body that is dead. New life can enter only in a new body. The old body must die before a new body can come into existence and a new life can enter into it. To put it simply, the old must cease to be operative before the new can begin to enliven and to pulsate. This is what I meant when I said you must discard the authority of the *Shastras* and destroy the religion of the *Shastras*.

## XXV

I have kept you too long. It is time I brought this address to a close. This would have been a convenient point for me to have stopped. But this would probably be my last address to a Hindu audience on a subject vitally concerning the Hindus. I would therefore like, before I close, to place before the Hindus, if they will allow me, some questions which I regard as vital and invite them seriously to consider the same.

In the first place, the Hindus must consider whether it is sufficient to take the placid view of the anthropologist that there is nothing to be said about the beliefs, habits, morals and outlooks on life, which obtain among the different peoples of the world except that they often differ; or whether it is not necessary to make an attempt to find out what kind of morality, beliefs, habits and outlook have worked best and have enabled those who possessed them to flourish, to go strong, to people the earth and to have dominion over it. As is observed by Prof. Carver, "Morality and religion, as the organised expression of moral approval and disapproval, must be regarded as factors in the struggle for existence as truly as are weapons for offence and defence, teeth and claws, horns and hoofs, furs and feathers. The social group, community, tribe or nation, which develops an unworkable scheme of morality or within which those social acts which weaken it and unfit it for survival, habitually create the sentiment of approval, while those which would strengthen and enable it to be expanded habitually create the sentiment of disapproval, will eventually be eliminated. It is its habits of approval or disapproval (these are the results of religion and morality) that handicap it, as really as the possession of two wings on one side with none on the other will handicap the colony of flies. It would be as futile in the one case as in the other to argue, that one system is just as good as another." Morality and religion, therefore, are not mere matters of likes and dislikes. You may dislike exceedingly a scheme of morality, which, if universally practised within a nation, would make that nation the strongest nation on the face of the earth. Yet in spite of your dislike such a nation will become strong. You may like exceedingly a scheme of morality and an ideal of justice, which if universally practised within a nation, would make it unable to hold its own in the struggle with other nations. Yet in spite of your admiration this nation will eventually disappear. The Hindus must, therefore, examine their religion and their morality in terms of their survival value.

*Secondly,* the Hindus must consider whether they should conserve the whole of their social heritage or select what is helpful and transmit to future generations only that much and no more. Prof. John Dewey, who was my teacher and to whom I owe so much, has said : "Every society gets encumbered with what is trivial, with dead wood from the past, and with what is positively perverse... As a society becomes more enlightened, it realizes that it is responsible *not* to conserve and transmit the whole of its existing achievements, but only such as make for a better future society." Even Burke, in spite of the vehemence with which he opposed the principle of change embodied in the French Revolution, was compelled to admit that "a State without the means of some change is without the means of its conservation. Without such means it might even risk the loss of that part of the constitution which it wished the most religiously to preserve." What Burke said of a State applies equally to a society.

*Thirdly,* the Hindus must consider whether they must not cease to worship the past as supplying its ideals. The beneful effect of this worship of the past are best summed up by Prof. Dewey when he says : "An individual can live only in the present. The present is not just something which comes after the past; much less something produced by it. It is what life is in leaving the past behind it. The study of past products will not help us to understand the present. A knowledge of the past and its heritage is of great significance when it enters into the present, but not otherwise. And the mistake of making the records and remains of the past the main material of education is that it tends to make the past a rival of the present and the present a more or less futile imitation of the past." The principle, which makes little of the present act of living and growing, naturally looks upon the present as empty and upon the future as remote. Such a principle is inimical to progress and is an hindrance to a strong and a steady current of life.

*Fourthly,* the Hindus must consider whether the time has not come for them to recognize that there is nothing fixed, nothing eternal, nothing *sanatan;* that everything is changing, that change is the law of life for individuals as well as for society. In a changing society, there must be a constant revolution of old values and the Hindus must realize that if there must be standards to measure the acts of men there must also be a readiness to revise those standards.

## XXVI

I have to confess that this address has become too lengthy. Whether this fault is compensated to any extent by breadth or depth is a matter for you to judge. All I claim is to have told you candidly my views. I have little to recommend them but some study and a deep concern in your destiny. If you will allow me to say, these views are the views of a man, who has been no tool of power, no flatterer of greatness. They come from one, almost the whole of whose public exertion has been one continuous struggle for liberty for the poor and for the oppressed and whose only reward has been a continuous shower of calumny and abuse from national journals and national leaders, for no other reason except that I refuse to join with them in performing the miracle—I will not say trick—of liberating the oppressed with the gold of the tyrant and raising the poor with the cash of the rich. All this may not be enough to commend my views. I think they are not likely to alter yours. But whether they do or do not, the responsibility is entirely yours. You must make your efforts to uproot Caste, if not in my way, then in your way. I am sorry, I will not be with you. I have decided to change. This is not the place for giving reasons. But even when I am gone out of your fold, I will watch your movement with active sympathy and you will have my assistance for what it may be worth. Yours is a national cause. Caste is no doubt primarily the breath of the Hindus. But the Hindus have fouled the air all over and everybody is infected, Sikh, Muslim and Christian. You, therefore, deserve the support of all those who are suffering from this infection, Sikh, Muslim and Christian. Yours is more difficult than the other national cause, namely Swaraj. In the fight for Swaraj you fight with the whole nation on your side. In this, you have to fight against the whole nation and that too, your own. But it is more important than Swaraj. There is no use having Swaraj, if you cannot defend it. More important than the question of defending Swaraj is the question of defending the Hindus under the Swaraj. In my opinion only when the Hindu Society becomes a casteless society that it can hope to have strength enough to defend itself. Without such internal strength, Swaraj for Hindus may turn out to be only a step towards slavery. Good-bye and good wishes for your success.

## APPENDIX I

## A VINDICATION OF CASTE BY MAHATMA GANDHI

(*A Reprint of his Articles in the "Harijan"*)

### Dr. Ambedkar's Indictment

### I

The readers will recall the fact that Dr. Ambedkar was to have presided last May at the annual conference of the Jat-Pat-Todak Mandal of Lahore. But the conference itself was cancelled because Dr. Ambedkar's address was found by the Reception Committee to be unacceptable. How far a Reception Committee is justified in rejecting a President of its choice because of his address that may be objectionable to it is open to question. The Committee knew Dr. Ambedkar's views on casts; and the Hindu scriptures. They knew also that he had in unequivocal terms decided to give up Hinduism. Nothing less than the address that Dr. Ambedkar had prepared was to be expected from him. The committee appears to have deprived the public of an opportunity of listening to the original views of a man, who has carved out for himself a unique position in society. Whatever label he wears in future, Dr. Ambedkar is not the man to allow himself to be forgotten.

Dr. Ambedkar was not going to be beaten by the Reception Committee. He has answered their rejection of him by publishing the address at his own expense. He has priced it at 8 annas, I would suggest a reduction to 2 annas or at least 4 annas.

No reformer can ignore the address. The orthodox will gain by reading it. This is not to say that the address is not open to objection. It has to be read only because it is open to serious objection. Dr. Ambedkar is a challenge to Hinduism. Brought up as a Hindu, educated by a Hindu potentate, he has become so disgusted with the so-called Savarna Hindus for the treatment that he and his people have received at their hands that he proposes to leave not only them but the very religion that is his and their common heritage. He has transferred to that religion, his disgust against a part of its professors.

But this is not to be wondered at. After all, one can only judge a system or an institution by the conduct of its representatives. What is more. Dr. Ambedkar found that the vast majority of Savarna Hindus had not only conducted themselves inhumanly against those of their fellow religionists, whom they classed as untouchables, but they had based their conduct on the authority of their scriptures, and when he began to search them he had found ample warrant for their beliefs in untouchability and all its implications. The author of the address has quoted chapter and verse in proof of his three-fold indictment—inhuman conduct itself, the unabashed justification for it on the part of the perpetrators, and the subsequent discovery that the justification was warranted by their scriptures.

No Hindu who prizes his faith above life itself can afford to underrate the importance of this indictment. Dr. Ambedkar is not alone in his disgust He is its most uncompromising exponent and one of the ablest among them. He is certainly the most irreconcilable among them. Thank God, in the front rank of the leaders, he is singularly alone and as yet but a representative of a very small minority. But what he says is voiced with more or less vehemence by many leaders belonging to the depressed classes. Only the latter, for instance Rao Bahadur M. C. Rajah and Dewan Bahadur Srinivasan, not only do not threaten to give up Hinduism but find enough warmth in it to compensate for the shameful persecution to which the vast mass of Harijans are exposed.

But the fact of many leaders remaining in the Hindu fold is no warrant for disregarding what Dr. Ambedkar has to say. The Savarnas have to correct their belief and their conduct. Above all those who are by their learning and influence among the Savarnas have to give an authoritative interpretation of the scriptures. The questions that Dr. Ambedkar's indictment suggest are :

(1) What are the scriptures ?

(2) Are all the printed texts to be regarded as an integral part of them or is any part of them to be rejected as unauthorised interpolations ?

(3) What is the answer of such accepted and expurgated scriptures on the question of untouchability, caste, equality of status, inter-dining and intermarriages ?

(These have been all examined by Dr. Ambedkar in his address.)

I must reserve for the next issue my own answer to these questions and a statement of the (at least some) manifest flaws in Dr. Ambedkar's thesis,

(*Harijan,* July 11, 1936)

## II

The *Vedas, Upanishads, Smritis* and *Puranas* including Ramayana and Mahabharata are the Hindu Scriptures. Nor is this a finite list. Every age or even generation has added to the list. It follows, therefore, that everything printed or even found handwritten is not scripture. The *Smritis* for instance contain much that can never be accepted as the word of God. Thus, many of the texts that Dr. Ambedkar quotes from the *Smritis* cannot be accepted as authentic. The scriptures, properly so-called, can only be concerned with eternal varieties and must appeal to any conscience *i.e.* any heart whose eyes of understanding are opened. Nothing can be accepted as the word of God which cannot be tested by reason or be capable of being spiritually experienced. And even when you have an expurgated edition of the scriptures, you will need their interpretation. Who is the best interpreter? Not learned men surely. Learning there must be. But religion does not live by it. It lives in the experiences of its saints and seers, in their lives and sayings. When all the most learned commentators of the scriptures are utterly forgotten, the accumulated experience of the sages and saints will abide and be an inspiration for ages to come.

Caste has nothing to do with religion. It is a custom whose origin I do not know and do not need to know for the satisfaction of my spiritual hunger. But I do know that it is harmful both to spiritual and national growth. *Varna* and *Ashrama* are institutions which have nothing to do with castes. The law of *Varna* teaches us that we have each one of us to earn our bread by following the ancestral calling. It defines not our rights but our duties. It necessarily has reference to callings that are conducive to the welfare of humanity and to no other. It also follows that there is no calling too low and none too high. All are good, lawful and absolutely equal in status. The callings of a Brahmin—spiritual teacher—and a scavenger are equal, and their due performance carries equal merit before God and at one time seems to have carried identical reward before man. Both were entitled to their livelihood and no more. Indeed one traces even now in the villages the faint lines of this healthy operation of the law. Living in Segaon with its population of 600, I do not find a great disparity between the earnings of different tradesmen including Brahmins. I find too that real Brahmins are to be found even in these degenerate days who are living on alms freely given to them and are giving freely of what they have of spiritual treasures. It would be wrong and improper to judge the law of *Varna* by its caricature in the lives of men who profess to belong to a *Varna,* whilst they openly commit a breach of its only operative rule. Arrogation of a superior status by and of the *Varna* over another is a denial of the law. And there is nothing in the law of *Varna* to warrant a belief in untouchability. (The essence of Hinduism is contained in its enunciation of one and only God as Truth and its bold acceptance of Ahimsa as the law of the human family.)

I am aware that my interpretation of Hinduism will be disputed by many besides Dr. Ambedkar. That does not affect my position. It is an interpretation by which I have lived for nearly half a century and according to which I have endeavoured to the best of my ability to regulate my life.

In my opinion the profound mistake that Dr. Ambedkar has made in his address is to pick out the texts of doubtful authenticity and value and the state of degraded Hindus who are no fit specimens of the faith they so woefully misrepresent. Judged by the standard applied by Dr. Ambedkar, every known living faith will probably fail.

In his able address, the learned Doctor has overproved his case- Can a religion that was professed by Chaitanya, Jnyandeo, Tukaram, Tiruvalluvar, Ramkrishna Paramahansa, Raja Rain Mohan Roy, Maharshi Devendranath Tagore, Vivekanand and host of others who might be easily mentioned, so utterly devoid of merit as is made out in Dr. Ambedkar's address ? A religion has to be judged not by its worst specimens but by the best it might have produced. For that and that alone can be used as the standard to aspire to, if not to improve upon.

(*Harijan,* July 18, 1936)

## III

## VARNA VERSUS CASTE

Shri Sant Ramji of the Jat-Pat-Todak Mandal of Lahore wants me to publish the following :

"I have read your remarks about Dr. Ambedkar and the Jat-Pat-Todak Mandal, Lahore. In that connection I beg to submit as follows :

"We did not invite Dr. Ambedkar to preside over our conference because he belonged to the Depressed Classes, for we do not distinguish between a touchable and an untouchable Hindu. On the contrary our choice fell on him simply because his diagnosis of the fatal disease of the Hindu community was the same as ours, *i.e.* he too was of the opinion that caste system was the root cause of the disruption and downfall of the Hindus. The subject of the Doctor's thesis for Doctorate being caste system, he has studied the subject thoroughly. Now the object of our conference was to pursuade the Hindus to annihilate castes but the advice of a non-Hindu in social and religious matters can have no effect on them. The Doctor in the supplementary portion of his address insisted on saying that that was his last speech as a Hindu, which was irrelevant as well as pernicious to the interests of the conference. So we requested him to expunge that sentence for he could easily say the same thing on any other occasion. But he refused and we saw no utility in making merely a show of our function. In spite of all this, I cannot help praising his address which is, as far as I know, the most learned thesis on the subject and worth translating into every vernacular of India.

Moreover, I want to bring to your notice that your philosophical difference between Caste and *Varna* is too subtle to be grasped by people in general, because for all practical purposes in the Hindu society Caste and *Varna* are one and the same thing, for the function of both of them is one and the same *i.e.* to restrict inter-caste marriages and inter-dining. Your theory of *Varnavyavastha* is impracticable in this age and there is no hope of its revival in the near future. But Hindus are slaves of caste and do not want to destroy it. So when you advocate your ideal of imaginary *Varnavyavastha* they find justification for clinging to caste. Thus you are doing a great disservice to social reform by advocating your imaginary utility of division of *Varnas,* for it creates hindrance in our way. To try to remove untouchability without striking at the root of *Varnavyavastha* is simply to treat the outward symptoms of a disease or to draw a line on the surface of water. As in the heart of their hearts *dvijas* do not want to give social equality to the so-called touchable and untouchable Shudras, so they refuse to break caste, and give liberal donations for the removal of untouchability, simply to evade the issue. To seek the help of the *Shastras* for the removal of untouchability and caste is simply to wash mud with mud."

The last paragraph of the letter surely cancels the first. If the Mandal rejects the help of the *Shastras,* they do exactly what Dr. Ambedkar does, *i.e.* cease to be Hindus. How then can they object to Dr. Ambedkar's address merely because he said that that was his last speech as a Hindu ? The position appears to be wholly untenable especially when the Mandal, for which , Shri Sant Ram claims to speak, applauds the whole argument of Dr. Ambedkar's address.

But it is pertinent to ask what the Mandal believes if it rejects the *Shastras.* How can a Muslim remain one if he rejects the Quran, or a Christian remain Christian if he rejects the Bible ? If Caste and *Varna* are convertible terms and if *Varna* is an integral part of the *Shastras* which define Hinduism, I do not know how a person who rejects Caste *i.e. Varna* can call himself a Hindu.

Shri Sant Ram likens the *Shastras* to mud. Dr. Ambedkar has not, so far as I remember, given any such pictures que name to the *Shastras*. I have certainly meant when I have said that if *Shastras* support the existing untouchability I should cease to call myself a Hindu. Similarly, if the *Shastras* support caste as we know it today in all its hideousness, I may not call myself or remain a Hindu since I have no scruples about interdining or intermarriage. I need not repeat my position regarding *Shastras* and their interpretation. I venture to suggest to Shri Sant Ram that it is the only rational and correct and morally defensible position and it has ample warrant in Hindu tradition.

*(Harijan,* August 15, 1936)

# APPENDIX II
# A REPLY TO THE MAHATMA BY DR. B.R. AMBEDKAR
## I

I appreciate greatly the honour done me by the Mahatma in taking notice in his Harijan of the speech on Caste which I had prepared for the Jat Pat Todak Mandal. From a perusal of his review of my speech it is clear that the Mahatma completely dissents from the views I have expressed on the subject of Caste. I am not in the habit of entering into controversy with my opponents unless there are special reasons which compel me to act otherwise. Had my opponent been some mean and obscure person I would not have pursued him. But my opponent being the Mahatma himself I feel I must attempt to meet the case to the contrary which he has sought to put forth. While I appreciate the honour he has done me, I must confess to a sense of surprize on finding that of all the persons the Mahatma should accuse me of a desire to seek publicity as he seems to do when he suggests that in publishing the undelivered speech my object was to see that I was not "forgotten". Whatever the Mahatma may choose to say my object in publishing the speech was to provoke the Hindus to think and take stock of their position. I have never hankered for publicity and if I may say so, I have more of it than I wish or need. But supposing it was out of the motive of gaining publicity that I printed the speech who could cast a stone at me ? Surely not those, who like the Mahatma live in glass houses.

## II

Motive apart, what has the Mahatma to say on the question raised by me in the speech ? First of all any one who reads my speech will realize that the Mahatma has entirely missed the issues raised by me and that the issues be has raised are not the issues that arise out of what he is pleased to call my indictment of the Hindus. The principal points which I have tried to make out in my speech may be catalogued as follows : (1) That caste has ruined the Hindus ; (2) That the reorganization of the Hindu society on the basis of Chaturvarnya is impossible because the *Varnavyavastha* is like a leaky pot or like a man running at the nose. It is incapable of sustaining itself by its own virtue and has an inherent tendency to degenerate into a caste system unless there is a legal sanction behind it which can be enforced against every one transgressing his *Varna* ; (3) That the reorganization of the Hindu Society on the basis of Chaturvarnya is harmful because the effect of the *Varnavyavastha* is to degrade the masses by denying them opportunity to acquire knowledge and to emasculate them by denying them the right to be armed ; (4) That the Hindu society must be reorganized on a religious basis which would recognise the principles of Liberty, Equality and Fraternity; (5) That in order to achieve this object the sense of religious sanctity behind

Caste and *Varna* must be destroyed ; (6) That the sanctity of Caste and *Varna* can be destroyed only by discarding the divine authority of the *Shastras*. It will be noticed that the questions raised by the Mahatma are absolutely beside the point and show that the main argument of the speech was lost upon him.

## III

Let me examine the substance of the points made by the Mahatma. The first point made by the Mahatma is that the texts cited by me are not authentic. I confess I am no authority on this matter. But I should like to state that the texts cited by me are all taken from the writings of the late Mr. Tilak who was a recognised authority on the Sanskrit language and on the Hindu *Shastras*. His second point is that these *Shastras* should be interpreted not by the learned but the saints and that, as the saints have understood them, the *Shastras* do not support Caste and Untouchability. As regards the first point what I like to ask the Mahatma is what does it avail to any one if the texts are interpolations and if they have been differently interpreted by the saints ? The masses do not make any distinction between texts which are genuine and texts which are interpolations. The masses do not know what the texts are. They are too illiterate to know the contents of the *Shastras*. They have believed what they have been told and what they have been told is that the *Shastras* do enjoin as a religious duty the observance of Caste and Untouchability.

With regard to the saints, one must admit that howsoever different and elevating their teachings may have been as compared to those of the merely learned they have been lamentably ineffective. They have been ineffective for two reasons. Firstly, none of the saints ever attacked the Caste System. On the contrary, they were staunch believers in the System of Castes. Most of them lived and died as members of the castes which they respectively belonged. So passionately attached was Jnyandeo to his status as a Brahmin that when the Brahmins of Paithan would not admit him to their fold he moved heaven and earth to get his status as a Brahmin recognized by the Brahmin fraternity. And even the saint Eknath who now figures in the film "Dharmatma" as a hero for having shown courage to touch the untouchables and dine with them, did so not because he was opposed to Caste and Untouchability but because he felt that the pollution caused thereby could be washed away by a bath in the sacred waters of the river Ganges.* The saints have never according to my study carried on a campaign against Caste and Untouchability. They were not concerned with the struggle between men. They were concerned with the relation between man and God. They did not preach that all men were equal. They preached that all men were equal in the eyes of God—

*अंत्यजाचा विटाळ ज्यासी । गंगास्नाने शुद्धत्व त्यासी ।।—**एकनाथी भागवत**, अ. २८, ओ.१९१.

a very different and a very innocuous proposition which nobody can find difficult to preach or dangerous to believe in. The second reason why the teachings of the saints proved ineffective was because the masses have been taught that a saint might break Caste but the common man must not. A saint therefore never became an example to follow. He always remained a pious man to be honoured. That the masses have remained staunch believers in Caste and Untouchability shows that the pious lives and noble sermons of the saints have had no effect on their life and conduct as against the teachings of the *Shastras*. Thus it can be a matter of no consolation that there were saints or that there is a Mahatma who understands the *Shastras* differently from the learned few or ignorant many. That the masses hold different view of the *Shastras* is fact which should and must be reckoned with. How is that to be dealt with except by denouncing the authority of the *Shastras,* which continue to govern their conduct, is a question which the Mahatma has not considered. But whatever the plan the Mahatma puts forth as an effective means to free the masses from the teachings of the *Shastras,* he must accept that the pious life led by one good Samaritan may be very elevating to himself but in India, with the attitude the common man has to saints and to Mahatmas—to honour but not to follow—one cannot make much out of it.

## IV

The third point made by the Mahatma is that a religion professed by Chaitanya, Jnyandeo, Tukaram, Tiruvalluvar, Ramkrishna Paramahansa etc. cannot be devoid of merit as is made out by me and that a religion has to be judged not by its worst specimens but by the best it might have produced. I agree with every word of this statement. But I do not quite understand what the Mahatma wishes to prove thereby. That religion should be judged not by its worst specimens but by its best is true enough but does it dispose of the matter ? I say it does not. The question still remains—why the worst number so many and the best so few ? To my mind there are two conceivable answers to this question : (1) That the worst by reason of some original perversity of theirs are morally uneducable and are therefore incapable of making the remotest approach to the religious ideal. Or (2) That the religious ideal is a wholly wrong ideal which has given a wrong moral twist to the lives of the many and that the best have become best in spite of the wrong ideal—in fact by giving to the wrong twist a turn in the right direction. Of these two explanations I am not prepared to accept the first and I am sure that even the Mahatma will not insist upon the contrary. To my mind the second is the only logical and reasonable explanation unless the Mahatma has a third alternative to explain why the worst are so many and the best so few. If the second is the only explanation then obviously the argument of the Mahatma that a religion should be judged by its best followers carries us nowhere except to pity the lot of the many who have gone wrong because they have been made to worship wrong ideals.

## V

The argument of the Mahatma that Hinduism would be tolerable if only many were to follow the example of the saints is fallacious for another reason.* By citing the names of such illustrious persons as Chaitanya etc. what the Mahatma seems to me to suggest in its broadest and simplest form is that Hindu society can be made tolerable and even happy without any fundamental change in its structure if all the high caste Hindus can be persuaded to follow a high standard of morality in their dealings with the low caste Hindus. I am totally opposed to this kind of ideology. I can respect those of the caste Hindus who try to realize a high social ideal in their life. Without such men India would be an uglier and a less happy place to live in than it is. But nonetheless anyone who relies on an attempt to turn the members of the caste Hindus into better men by improving their personal character is in my judgment wasting his energy and hugging an illusion. Can personal character make the maker of armaments a good man, *i.e.* a man who will sell shells that will not burst and gas that will not poison? If it cannot, how can you accept personal character to make a man loaded with the consciousness of Caste, a good man, *i.e.* a man who would treat his fellows as his friends and equals? To be true to himself he must deal with his fellows either as a superior or inferior according as the case may be; at any rate, differently from his own caste fellows. He can never be expected to deal with his fellows as his kinsmen and equals. As a matter of fact, a Hindu does treat all those who are not of his Caste as though they were aliens, who could be discriminated against with impunity and against whom any fraud or trick may be practised without shame. *This is to say that there can be a better or a worse Hindu. But a good Hindu there cannot be.* This is so not because there is anything wrong with his personal character. In fact what is wrong is the entire basis of his relationship to his fellows. The best of men cannot be moral if the basis of relationship between them and their fellows is fundamentally a wrong relationship. To a slave his master may be better or worse. But there cannot be a good master. A good man cannot be a master and a master cannot be a good man. The same applies to the relationship between high caste and low caste. To a low caste man a high caste man can be better or worse as compared to other high caste men. A high caste man cannot be a good man in so far as he must have a low caste man to distinguish him as high caste man. It cannot be good to a low caste man to be conscious that there is a high caste man above him. I have argued in my speech that a society based on *Varna* or Caste is a society which is based on a wrong relationship. I had hoped that the Mahatma would attempt to demolish my argument. But instead of doing that he has merely reiterated his belief in Chaturvarnya without disclosing the ground on which it is based

---

* In this connection see illuminating article on *Morality and the Social Structure* by Mr. H. N. Brailsford in the Aryan Path for April 1936.

## VI

Does the Mahatma practise what he preaches ? One does not like to make personal reference in an argument which is general in its application. But when one preaches a doctrine and holds it as a dogma there is a curiosity to know how far he practises what he preaches. It may be that his failure to practise is due to the ideal being too high to be attainable ; it may be that his failure to practise is due to the innate hypocracy of the man. In any case he exposes his conduct to examination and I must not be blamed if I asked how far has the Mahatma attempted to realize his ideal in his own case. The Mahatma is a Bania by birth. His ancestors had abandoned trading in favour of ministership which is a calling of the Brahmins. In his own life, before he became a Mahatma, when occasion came for him to choose his career he preferred law to scales. On abandoning law he became half saint and half politician. He has never touched trading which is his ancestral calling. His youngest son—I take one who is a faithful follower of his father—born a Vaishya has married a Brahmin's daughter and has chosen to serve a newspaper magnate. The Mahatma is not known to have condemned him for not following his ancestral calling. It may be wrong and uncharitable to judge an ideal by its worst specimens. But surely the Mahatma as a specimen has no better and if he even fails to realize the ideal then the ideal must be an impossible ideal quite opposed to the practical instincts of man. Students of Carlyle know that he often spoke on a subject before he thought about it. I wonder whether such has not been the case with the Mahatma in regard to the subject matter of Caste. Otherwise certain questions which occur to me would not have escaped him. When can a calling be deemed to have become an ancestral calling so as to make it binding on a man ? Must man follow his ancestral calling even if it does not suit his capacities, even when it has ceased to be profitable ? Must a man live by his ancestral calling even if he finds it to be immoral ? If every one must pursue his ancestral calling then it must follow that a man must continue to be a pimp because his grandfather was a pimp and a woman must continue to be a prostitute because her grandmother was a prostitute. Is the Mahatma prepared to accept the logical conclusion of his doctrine ? To me his ideal of following one's ancestral calling is not only an impossible and impractical ideal, but it is also morally an indefensible ideal.

## VII

The Mahatma sees great virtue in a Brahmin remaining a Brahmin all his life. Leaving aside the fact there are many Brahmins who do not like to remain Brahmins all their lives. What can we say about those Brahmins who have clung to their ancestral calling of priesthood ? Do they do so from any faith in the virtue of the principle of ancestral calling or do they do so from motives of filthy lucre ? The Mahatma does not seem to concern himself with such queries. He is satisfied that these are "real Brahmins who are living on alms freely given to them and giving freely what they have of spiritual treasures". This is how a hereditary Brahmin priest appears to the Mahatma—a carrier of spiritual treasures. But another portrait of the hereditary Brahmin can also be drawn. A Brahmin can be a priest to Vishnu—the God of Love. He can be a priest to Shankar—the God of Destruction. He can be a priest at Buddha Gaya worshipping Buddha—the greatest teacher of mankind who taught the noblest doctrine of Love. He also can be a priest to Kali, the Goddess, who must have a daily sacrifice of an animal to satisfy her thirst for blood ; He will be a priest of the temple of Rama—the Kshatriya God! He will also be a priest of the Temple of Parshuram, the God who took Avatar to destroy the Kshatriyas ! He can be a priest to Bramha, the Creator of the world. He can be a priest to a Pir whose God Allah will not brook the claim of Bramha to share his spiritual dominion over the world! No one can say that this is a picture which is not true to life. If this is a true picture one does not know what to say of this capacity to bear loyalties to Gods and Goddesses whose attributes are so antagonistic that no honest man can be a devotee to all of them. The Hindus rely upon this extraordinary phenomenon as evidence of the greatest virtue of their religion—namely its catholicity, its spirit of toleration. As against this facile view, it can be urged that what is toleration and catholicity may be really nothing more creditable than indifference or flaccid latitudinarianism. These two attitudes are hard to distinguish in their outer seeming. But they are so vitally unlike in their real quality that no one who examines them closely can mistake one for the other. That a man is ready to render homage to many Gods and Goddesses may be cited as evidence of his tolerant spirit. But can it not also be evidence of insincerity born of a desire to serve the times ? I am sure that this toleration is merely insincerity. If this view is well founded, one may ask what spiritual treasure can there be with a person who is ready to be a priest and a devotee to any deity which it serves his purpose to worship and to adore ? Not only must such a person be deemed to be bankrupt of all spiritual treasures but for him to practice so elevating a profession as that of a priest simply because it is ancestral, without faith, without belief, moroly as a mechanical process handed down from father to son, is not a conservation of virtue; it is really the prostitution of a noble profession which is no other than the service of religion.

## VIII

Why does the Mahatma cling to the theory of every one following his or her ancestral calling ? He gives his reasons nowhere. But there must be some reason although he does not care to avow it. Years ago writing on "Caste *versus* Class" in his *Young India* he argued that Caste System was better than Class System on the ground that caste was the best possible adjustment of social stability. If that be the reason why the Mahatma clings to the theory of every one following his or her ancestral calling, then he is clinging to a false view of social life. Everybody wants social stability and some adjustment must be made in the relationship between individuals and classes in order that stability may be had. But two things, I am sure nobody wants. One thing nobody wants is static relationship, something that is unalterable, something that is fixed for all times. Stability is wanted but not at the cost of change when change is imperative. Second thing nobody wants is mere adjustment. Adjustment is wanted but not at the sacrifice of social justice. Can it be said that the adjustment of social relationship on the basis of caste *i.e.* on the basis of each to his hereditary calling avoids these two evils ? I am convinced that it does not. Far from being the best possible adjustment I have no doubt that it is of the worst possible kind inasmuch as it offends against both the canons of social adjustment—namely fluidity and equity.

## IX

Some might think that the Mahatma has made much progress inasmuch as he now only believes in *Varna* and does not believe in Caste. It is true that there was a time when the Mahatma was a full-blooded and a blue-blooded Sanatani Hindu. He believed in the *Vedas*, the *Upanishads*, the *Puranas* and all that goes by the name of Hindu scriptures and therefore in *avatars* and rebirth. He believed in Caste and defended it with the vigour of the orthodox. He condemned the cry for inter-dining, inter-drinking and inter-marrying and argued that restraints about inter-dining to a great extent "helped the cultivation of will-power and the conservation of certain social virtue". It is good that he has repudiated this sanctimonious nonsense and admitted that caste "is harmful both to spiritual and national growth," and may be, his son's marriage outside his caste has had something to do with this change of view. But has the Mahatma really progressed ? What is the nature of the *Varna* for which the Mahatma stands ? Is it the *Vedic* conception as commonly understood and preached by Swami Dayanand Saraswati and his followers, the Arya Samajists ? The essence of the *Vedic* conception of *Varna* is the pursuit of a calling which is appropriate to one's natural aptitude. The essence of the Mahatma's conception of *Varna* is the pursuit of ancestral calling irrespective of natural aptitude. What is the difference between Caste and *Varna* as understood by the Mahatma ? I find none. As defined by the Mahatma, *Varna* becomes merely a different name for Caste for the simple reason that it is the same in essence—namely pursuit of ancestral calling. Far from making progress the Mahatma has suffered retrogression. By putting this interpretation upon the *Vedic* conception of *Varna* he has really made ridiculous what was sublime. While I reject the *Vedic Varnavyavastha* for reasons given in the speech I must admit that the *Vedic* theory of *Varna* as interpreted by Swami Dayanand and some others is a sensible and an inoffensive thing. It did not admit birth as a determining factor in fixing the place of an individual in society. It only recognized worth. The Mahatma's view of *Varna* not only makes nonsense of the *Vedic Varna* but it makes it an abominable thing. *Varna* and Caste are two very different concepts. *Varna* is based on the principle of each according to his worth-while Caste is based on the principle of each according to his birth. The two are as distinct as chalk is from cheese. In fact there is an antithesis between the two. If the Mahatma believes as he does in every one following his or her ancestral calling, then most certainly he is advocating the Caste System and that in calling it the *Varna* System he is not only guilty of terminological inexactitude, but he is causing confusion worse confounded. I am sure that all his confusion is due to the fact that the Mahatma has no definite and clear conception as to what is *Varna* and what is Caste and as to the necessity of either for the conservation of Hinduism. He has said and one hopes that he will not find some mystic reason to change his view that caste is not the essence of Hinduism. Does he regard *Varna* as the essence of Hinduism ? One cannot as yet give any categorical answer. Readers of his article on "Dr. Ambedkar's Indictment" will answer "No". In that article he does not say that the dogma of *Varna* is an essential part of the creed of Hinduism. Far from making *Varna* the essence of Hinduism he says "the essence of Hinduism is contained in its enunciation of one and only God as Truth and its bold acceptance of Ahimsa as the law of the human family" But the readers of his article in reply to Mr. Sant Ram will say "Yes". In that article he says "How can a Muslim remain one if he rejects the Quran, or a Christian remain as Christian if he rejects the Bible ? If Caste and *Varna* are convertible terms and if *Varna* is an integral part of the *Shastras* which define Hinduism I do not know how a person who rejects Caste, *i.e. Varna* can call himself a Hindu ?" Why this prevarication ? Why does the Mahatma hedge ? Whom does he want to please ? Has the saint failed to sense the truth ? Or does the politician stand in the way of the Saint ? The real reason why the Mahatma is suffering from this confusion is probably to be traced to two sources. The first is the temperament of the Mahatma. He has almost in everything the simplicity of the child with the child's capacity for self-deception. Like a child he can believe in anything he wants to believe. We must therefore wait till such time as it pleases the Mahatma to abandon his faith in *Varna* as it has pleased him to abandon his faith in Caste. The second source of confusion is the double role which the Mahatma wants to play—of a Mahatma and a Politician. As a Mahatma he may be trying to spiritualize Politics. Whether he has succeeded in it or not Politics have certainly commercialized him. A politician must knew that Society cannot bear the whole truth and that he must not speak the whole truth; if he is speaking the whole truth it is bad for his politics. The reason why the Mahatma is always supporting Caste and *Varna* is because he is afraid that if he opposed them he will lose his place in politics. Whatever may be the source of this confusion the

Mahatma must be told that he is deceiving himself and also deceiving the people by preaching Caste under the name of *Varna*.

## X

The Mahatma says that the standards I have applied to test Hindus and Hinduism are too severe and that judged by those standards every known living faith will probably fail. The complaint that my standards are high may be true. But the question is not whether they are high or whether they are low. The question is whether they are the right standards to apply. A People and their Religion must be judged by social standards based on social ethics. No other standard would have any meaning if religion is held to be a necessary good for the well-being of the people. Now I maintain that the standards I have applied to test Hindus and Hinduism are the most appropriate standards and that I know of none that are better. The conclusion that every known religion would fail if tested by my standards may be true. But this fact should not give the Mahatma as the champion of Hindus and Hinduism a ground for comfort any more than the existence of one madman should give comfort to another madman or the existence of one criminal should give comfort to another criminal. I like to assure the Mahatma that it is not the mere failure of the Hindus and Hinduism which has produced in me the feelings of disgust and contempt with which I am charged. I realize that the world is a very imperfect world and any one who wants to live in it must bear with its imperfections. But while I am prepared to bear with the imperfections and shortcomings of the society in which I may be destined to labour, I feel I should not consent to live in a society which cherishes wrong ideals or a society which having right ideals will not consent to bring its social life in conformity with those ideals. If I am disgusted with Hindus and Hinduism it is because I am convinced that they cherish wrong ideals and live a wrong social life. My quarrel with Hindus and Hinduism is not over the imperfections of their social conduct. It is much more fundamental. It is over their ideals.

## XI

Hindu society seems to me to stand in need of a moral regeneration which it is dangerous to postpone. And the question is who can determine and control this moral regeneration ? Obviously only those who have undergone an intellectual regeneration and those who are honest enough to have the courage of their convictions born of intellectual emancipation. Judged by this standard the Hindu leaders who count are in my opinion quite unfit for the task. It is impossible to say that they have undergone the preliminary intellectual regeneration. If they had undergone an intellectual regeneration they would neither delude themselves in the simple way of the untaught multitude nor would they take advantage of the primitive ignorance of others as one sees them doing. Notwithstanding the crumbling state of Hindu society these leaders, will nevertheless unblushingly appeal to ideals of the past which have in every way ceased to have any connection with the present; which however suitable they might have been in the days of their origin have now become a warning rather than a guide. They still have a mystic respect for the earlier forms which make them disinclined—nay opposed to any examination of the foundations of their Society. The Hindu masses are of course incredibly heedless in the formation of their beliefs. But so are the Hindu leaders. And what is worse is that these Hindu leaders become filled with an illicit passion for their beliefs when any one proposes to rob them of their companionship. The Mahatma is no exception. The Mahatma appears not to believe in thinking. He prefers to follow the saints. Like a conservative with his reverence for consecrated notions he is afraid that if he once starts thinking, many ideals and institutions to which he clings wilt be doomed. One must sympathize with him. For every act of independent thinking puts some portion of apparently stable world in peril. But it is equally true that dependence on saints cannot lead us to knew the truth. The saints are after all only human beings and, as Lord Balfour said, "the human mind is no more a truth finding apparatus than the snout of a pig". In so far as he does think, to me he really appears to be prostituting his intelligence to find reasons for supporting this archaic social structure of the Hindus. He is the most influential apologist of it and therefore the worst enemy of the Hindus.

Unlike the Mahatma there are Hindu leaders who arc not content merely to believe and follow. They dare to think, and act in accordance with the result of their thinking. But unfortunately they are cither a dishonest lot or an indifferent lot when it comes to the question of giving right guidance to the mass of the people. Almost every Brahmin has transgressed the rule of Caste. The number of Brahmins who sell shoes is far greater than those who practise priesthood. Not only have the Brahmins given up their ancestral calling of priesthood for trading but they have entered trades which are prohibited to them by the *Shastras*. Yet how many Brahmins who break Caste every day will preach against Caste and against the *Shastras*? For one honest Brahmin preaching against Caste and *Shastras* because his practical instinct and moral conscience cannot support a conviction in them, there are hundreds who break Caste and trample upon the *Shastras* every day but who are the most fanatic upholders of the theory of Caste and the sanctity of the *Shastras*. Why this duplicity? Because they feel that if the masses are emancipated from the yoke of Caste they would be a menace to the power and prestige of the Brahmins as a class. The dishonesty of this intellectual class who would deny the masses the fruits of their thinking is a most disgraceful phenomenon.

The Hindus in the words of Mathew Arnold are "wandering between two worlds, one dead, the other powerless to be born". What are they to do? The

Mahatma to whom they appeal for guidance does not believe in thinking and can therefore give no guidance which can be said to stand the test of experience. The intellectual classes to whom the masses look for guidance are either too dishonest or too indifferent to educate them in the right direction. We are indeed witnesses to a great tragedy. In the face of this tragedy all one can do is to lament and say—such be thy Leaders, O! Hindus.

●●

## About the Author

Bhim Rao was born in Mhow, Madhya Pradesh, to Ramji Maloji Sakpal and Bhimabai on April 14, 1891; Bhimrao's ancestors belonged to the Mahar caste, who were guerrillas in the army of Maharaja Shivaji. Although the Mahar caste was considered the lowest in the society, they were equal to Kshatriyas in fighting spirit. As a child, he was passionate about cricket and music. Ambedkar, a Brahmin who taught Bhim Rao in School, added his family name to Bhimrao's name. The Constitution of India was the brainchild of Ambedkar, who was educated at the famous Elphinstone College in Bombay, then at Columbia University in the United States, the London School of Economics, and the prestigious Gray's Inn in London. An expert in Economics, Law, and Politics equally, he was a staunch opponent of the Aryan invasion theory. In his books, he wrote extensively on the caste system, Islamic fundamentalism, and organized conversion. Ambedkar, a staunch patriot in his Ph.D. dissertation, sharply criticized the British economic policies that led to India's economic collapse. He came up with adding the Ashoka Chakra to India's national flag. He is the first and only person in the world to graduate as a Doctor of All Sciences from the London School of Economics. Furthermore, he spent 16 to 21 hours a day studying. Ambedkar's research paper on economics at the London School of Economics paved the Reserve Bank of India's policies. In his research paper, he expounded on the devaluation of the rupee and demonetization. Ambedkar was the first backward class lawyer in the country and the first backward caste student to study abroad. He had a profound knowledge of 64 subjects and was an expert in nine languages, including French, German, Persian, and Sanskrit. The Government of India pronounced him as the most excellent scholar the world has ever seen. He became the first law minister in Independent and later resigned from the ministry following a disagreement with Prime Minister Nehru. He died on December 6, 1956, at the age of 65. The Bharat Ratna was awarded to him by the VP Singh-led government in 1990, 35 years after his death, because he was unacceptable to the Nehru-Gandhi family due to his differences with Nehru.